EASY READING
SHAKESPEARE
VOLUME THREE

By the same author:

Easy Reading Shakespeare Volume One: The Bard in Bite-Size Verse, The Book Guild, 2005

Easy Reading Shakespeare Volume Two: The Bard in Bite-Size Verse, The Book Guild, 2006

Kenneth Grahame's The Wind in the Willows in Bite-Size Verse, The Book Guild, 2005

EASY READING
SHAKESPEARE
VOLUME THREE

The Bard in Bite-Size Verse

Richard Cuddington

Book Guild Publishing
Sussex, England

First published in Great Britain in 2006 by
The Book Guild Ltd
Pavilion View
19 New Road,
Brighton,
BN1 1UF

Typesetting in Times by
Keyboard Services, Luton, Bedfordshire

Printed in Great Britain by
Antony Rowe Ltd, Chippenham, Wiltshire

A catalogue record for this book is available from
The British Library

ISBN 1 84624 059 X

For Reg and Barbara Barcock

CONTENTS

Then finally he dragged himself
Up out and through the mud

THE MERRY WIVES OF WINDSOR

Sir John Falstaff, old fat Jack –
Someone I'm sure you know –
Has just developed an idea
To make himself some dough.

He's short of ready funds and says,
'I think I'll have a bash
At carrying out a scheme I have
To make some ready cash.'

Of course he's no intention
Of working very hard;
This wouldn't suit old Jack at all,
That huge great lump of lard.

This lecherous and lazy knight,
This greedy, lying rogue
Smiled to himself and archly said
In his deep, winning brogue,

'I'll use my manly bluster
And all my crafty wiles
And good old Jack's most charming ways
And his most winning smiles

'To prosecute a marvellous plan
That will ensure I get
A load of readies in my hands' –
And thus his scheme was set.

And so this stout old reprobate,
This reveller, this clown,
Proceeds upon his sneaky way
To good old Windsor town.

He'd pondered 'get rich' schemes before,
But now he thought, 'I'm blest!
For this one's quite a cracker,
One of my very best.'

He'd come to Windsor with some friends,
For Mistress Quickly's there;
Both Nym and Pistol go with him
And they intend to share

In all the fun and good old times
Their master always makes,
For he won't stop at anything –
He'll do just what it takes

To entertain the ladies;
He'll have a drink or two,
Or anything that seems like fun:
That's what this knight will do.

This reveller, this clown

So Jack is now ensconced within
The noisy Garter Inn
And outlines his ambitious plan
Above the merry din.

He says, 'There's wives in Windsor,
I swear, that fancy me.
It doesn't take much working out
For me to clearly see

'That Mrs Ford is really keen;
I'm sure she holds me dear.
I saw her gaze at me and give
A most "come hither" leer,

'Which truly made it very plain
Her heart was fit to melt,
For I could see in just a tick
How this poor woman felt.

'And Mrs Page examined me
In Windsor, yesterday,
Just like she was undressing me
In such a brazen way.

'And so I think I know for sure
What's on the lady's mind,
For I'm an expert after all
On all of womankind.'

So Jack is now ensconced within
The noisy Garter Inn

So this is Falstaff's clever plan,
What he decides to do:
'Both Mrs Ford and Mrs Page
I do intend to woo,

'For I have heard they both are wed
To men who each lay claim
To having massive fortunes – so
This now will be my game:

'To win the hearts of these two wives,
For I've been given word
They have free access to these funds –
At least that's what I've heard.'

What a devious, artful chap!
A villain to be sure –
Up for any rotten trick,
Outside or in the law.

And now he plans to woo these two.
He really thinks he'll win
Their hearts and minds and their true love –
What world does he live in?

When was the last time that he looked
At his debauched old face,
Or down at his enormous gut
Which is a sad disgrace?

A long look in the mirror
Might just have made him think
That he was wasting all his time –
He'd give up in a wink,

All plans of winning their sweet hearts;
But no – poor sad old Jack
Thinks he's a handsome fellow as
He drinks his glass of sack.

And so he writes two letters,
And both missives are the same,
Except that he addresses them
With each a different name.

To Mrs Ford he'll send the one –
And one to Mrs Page.
But then old Falstaff gets into
A monumental rage,

For Nym and Pistol whom he asks
To carry these two notes
Refuse to get involved and so
He grabs their scrawny throats.

But still this won't persuade them;
They say they just feel tired...
And so Jack Falstaff tells them both,
'The pair of you are fired!'

In anger and resentment then
Towards their boss, old Jack,
They both make up their minds to get
Revenge and pay him back.

So Pistol goes to Mr Ford –
He says, 'I've come to say
Sir John has sent a letter to
Your own sweet wife today.

'And in it he avows his love;
I swear upon my life
That Falstaff, that old scoundrel,
Is set to have your wife.'

Now Ford was fiery in his way
And of a jealous turn,
So when he heard of this device
His rage began to burn.

And there and then, within his heart,
He vowed he'd set a trap
To catch old Falstaff in the act.
He'd teach the cheeky chap!

Nym made his way to Mr Page
And to that worthy said,
'Falstaff is doing all he can
To get your wife in bed.'

But Mr Page laughed merrily
When of this plan he learned;
He trusted her implicitly,
So he was not concerned.

Then Ford and Page discussed it all
And both of them agreed
They wouldn't tell their wives they knew –
They saw no pressing need.

⁓ཚ⁓

But as the husbands heard the news
The wives received word too,
Contained in Falstaff's letters which
Professed a love so true,

A passion burning in the heart
Of that conceited bloke.
Heaven knows what all this meant!
Was it some kind of joke?

The ladies were astounded
When each of them compared
The letters filled with fervent words
That these epistles shared.

Contained within each letter,
To make the matter worse,
Were badly phrased and clumsy
Attempts at rhyming verse.

The ladies were amazed, amused,
And shocked – but both agreed
A lesson should be taught for this
Impertinent misdeed.

And they began to giggle as
They hatched a cunning plan
To have some laughs at the expense
Of this conceited man.

They said, 'We'll make the silly fool,
That fat old greasy knight,
Believe we find his drunken face
A very welcome sight.

'We'll make him think we love to see
His lovelorn, leering glances.
Yes, we'll convince the stupid ass
We yearn for his advances.

'We'll make him think his sodden face
Is welcome like the sun...
And thus, without a trace of doubt,
We'll really have some fun.'

One further thing they then agreed,
And that was not to tell
Their husbands what they planned to do,
Since Ford, for one, would yell,

And carry on in such a way
And let off so much steam
That he would very likely spoil
This smashing, fun-filled scheme.

They went to Mistress Quickly,
And involved her in their plan;
They told her everything they had
In store for this fat man.

Then Mistress Quickly up and went,
As one of this accord,
To tell Sir John what time was best
To visit Mrs Ford.

'Her husband will be out when you
Have heard the clock strike ten.
Mrs Ford says, "Come to her,
And make your visit then."

'And by the way, my master dear,
I've also heard it said
That Mrs Page loves you as well,
You've really turned her head.'

Well, foolish Falstaff beamed and thought,
'I am *the* man – by gad!
A gift to all the ladies fair,
A bold and handsome lad.'

So later on he made his way,
Dressed up just like a lord,
Exuding confidence and charm,
To call on Mrs Ford.

The wives are waiting for him
And they have hatched a plan
That's guaranteed to make a fool
Of this absurd old man.

He knocks – and Mrs Page runs off
Within the house to hide,
While Mrs Ford, with many a grin,
Now ushers him inside.

'Oh, sweet Sir John, why there you are.'
She gathers up her skirts
And says, 'Come in at once, my dear.'
And brazenly she flirts.

He says, 'My heavenly jewel fair,
You're everything to me.
For you I'd cross a desert vast
Or swim across the sea.'

But Mrs Ford looks down, goes red,
And says, 'That's what you say,
But is it true what you profess?
Please answer this, I pray.'

She adds, 'You know, I think you love
That Mrs Page much more...
And thinking this has really cut
Your sweetheart to the core.'

'Oh, not at all,' the fat knight cried.
His voice was full of scorn.
'You are the only one for me.'
He tried to sound lovelorn.

'For I'm enraptured by your face,
Your lovely eyes, your hair.
That Mrs Page is plain and thin
And really can't compare

'With you, my lovely Mrs Ford.
I couldn't love you more.'
But as he spoke a servant then
Appeared there at the door.

'Mrs Page is coming now,'
The servant loudly cried.
This was of course part of the plan
To take Jack for a ride.

He runs to hide as Mrs Page
Comes rushing in and cries,
'You're with Jack Falstaff, I'll be bound –
And don't go telling lies.'

Mrs Ford admits the truth;
(The girls are having fun.)
Then Mrs Page says, 'You'd best tell
John Falstaff there, to run,

'Because your husband's on his way –
He'll be here in a flash.
The best thing that Sir John can do
Is try to make a dash.'

But no – it really is too late:
That's what they tell Sir John.
The plan is going very well –
Of course, it's just a con.

So out of hiding Falstaff comes.
'Oh help me please,' he said.
'Your husband's sure to challenge me
And I might end up dead.'

'You'll have to hide,' the ladies cried.
'It's all there is to do.
Get in this laundry basket here.
We'll take good care of you.'

They stuffed him in the basket
With dirty pants and socks

They stuffed him in the basket
With dirty pants and socks,
With greasy napkins, grubby ruffs,
Foul-smelling shirts and smocks.

What a profound indignity
For this vainglorious knight.
They said, 'It is imperative
That you keep out of sight.'

Once Falstaff was well hidden
With garments to his chin,
They fastened down the basket lid
And called some servants in.

Two men arrived and Mrs Ford
In shrieking voice then cried,
'Remove this smelly basket here.
Please take the thing outside

'And throw it in the River Thames,
I'll have it here no more.'
Falstaff, in hiding, didn't hear
What fate he had in store.

And so the two men carried
The basket to the bank.
They threw it in the river, where
It very quickly sank.

Well, old fat Jack trapped there inside
Fought hard and pushed his way
Through dirty knickers, filthy rags,
And sheets all grimy grey,

Till finally his head popped out,
All soaking wet and cold.
He didn't look a valiant knight;
He just looked grey and old.

He spluttered, wheezed and coughed and sneezed,
He floundered, fought and blew
Great spouts of water from his mouth,
Tried every trick he knew

To get his blubber and his bulk
Safe back onto the shore,
And as he did he shouted out
And cursed aloud and swore.

Then finally he dragged himself
Up out and through the mud,
Through slimy weed and clinging dirt,
Through all the muck and crud.

And standing on the bank he looked
Upon the dirty river,
Then turned his back and made his way,
Depressed and with a shiver,

And standing on the bank he looked
Upon the dirty river

Towards the Garter Inn – and there,
As soon as he got back,
He yelled out with a mighty roar,
'Bring me a quart of sack!'

Then, once he had recovered,
He said, 'I tell you all,
I'll never cook up schemes again
Whatever may befall.

'I won't dream up these silly plans
In all my life again.
I never shall expose myself
To mockery and pain.

'I'm through with all this fooling,
I shan't do anymore' –
But as he spoke Miss Quickly
Came striding through the door.

'Mrs Ford says she regrets
You wound up getting wet;
She says she'll make it up to you –
She'll make you love her yet.

'So, with apologies, she hopes
You now are feeling fine –
And will you come tomorrow
Sometime 'twixt eight and nine?'

Well, Falstaff sat bolt upright then.
He said, 'It's my old charm.
Yes, I'll be there you can be sure,
For it can do no harm.'

And so he made his way again,
Now feeling more assured,
To see the lady he desired,
To call on Mrs Ford.

But when he gets there, he is told,
Just as he was before,
That Mrs Page is on her way –
But then there's worse in store.

For once again he hears that Ford,
Who fills him full of fear,
Is striding through old Windsor town
And even then draws near.

Mrs Ford cries, 'Hide again!
The basket's by the chair.'
Falstaff cries out desperately,
'I'll not get back in there.'

'Well, then we must disguise you.
Here, put these garments on.'
When Falstaff looked he cried aloud,
'I really cannot don

'Habiliments like these – they are
A fat old woman's gear.'
But he was soon persuaded when
They said that Ford drew near.

The clothes belonged to some old dame
Who'd come from Brainford town,
And when she'd gone she'd left behind
This coloured, cotton gown.

The dress was huge, a perfect fit
For stout old Falstaff there,
But what he wasn't told was that
He really should beware,

For Mr Ford just couldn't stand
The Brainford woman, so
It would have been a useful thing
For poor old Jack to know.

While he was busy changing
Mr Ford came rushing in.
He thought that Falstaff might be there,
Committing carnal sin.

He grabbed the laundry basket,
And threw it 'cross the floor;
He tossed the clothes around the room
And then he loudly swore,

That he believed Jack Falstaff
Was there to see his wife.
He said, 'If that old rogue is here,
I swear I'll take his life.'

But then an apparition
Comes waddling down the stairs,
And in a moment Mr Ford
Forgot his other cares.

The man was wholly taken in.
He thought, 'That Brainford bitch!
I really hate her and I'm sure
That she's some kind of witch.'

He grabbed his heavy walking stick.
'I'll not have this,' he swore.
And with the most almighty blows
Drove Falstaff out the door.

Now, after he had disappeared
The wives told everyone
About the scheme they'd put in place,
How they had had such fun,

But then an apparition
Comes waddling down the stairs

Humiliating foolish Jack.
He'd got what he deserved.
'He is an ugly, silly man,'
Good Mrs Ford observed.

Her husband, now he'd heard the truth,
Remorsefully he spoke:
'I'm sorry I mistrusted you
About that stupid bloke.'

And then they all began to weave
Another devious plan,
To once again humiliate
That vain, flirtatious man.

They all agreed it would be fun
To have one final go
At making Falstaff look a fool,
Teach him a lesson ... so

They planned thus to entice the knight
To Windsor forest where
There is a legend that says all
Should take the greatest care,

For dreadful 'Herne the Hunter',
Whom everybody fears,
From time to time with ragged horns
Within the wood appears.

He causes great destruction,
He runs and goes amok –
And here it is they plan to make
Sir John a laughing stock.

They gathered lots of children, and
To make them pretty scary
They dressed each child to look just like
A nymph or woodland fairy.

They hope to make the bumptious knight
Quite frightened by this plan,
When all these fairies there accost
The unsuspecting man.

So Mistress Quickly goes to him
And says, 'The two good wives
Desire that you will come to them –
They love you with their lives.

'Please meet them in the forest,
They're waiting for you there.'
So daft Sir John sets off right then
With not the slightest care.

He meets them, and he's thinking,
'I've cracked it with this pair.'
But then a mighty crashing noise
Gives both the wives a scare.

They rush into the forest;
The fairies then appear.
Falstaff crouches by a tree,
And trembles there with fear.

He watches as they dance around –
A sight he's never seen.
The man is truly terrified.
Whatever does this mean?

And as he tries to hide he says,
'I hope they don't see me.'
But then one of the 'fairies' cries,
'Who's there behind that tree?'

They drag him out into the glade
And push and pull him round;
They pinch him and then punch him too –
He falls upon the ground.

Tormenting him with mild abuse,
Some also burn his skin,
And then they pull him round and round,
All dizzy in a spin.

They pluck some flowers and with them write,
As Falstaff stands and blinks,
A motto saying, 'Evil comes
To him who evil thinks'.

They warn poor Falstaff then against
His sinful fantasy
Of lustful and of shameful thoughts –
And he begins to see,

The error of his ways and how
He's really been quite bad,
That he has been a selfish knight,
A stupid, daft old cad.

And just as he was thinking,
'I can't take all this stuff',
The adults who'd been hiding felt
The knight had had enough.

They stepped out from the forest
And stopped all the abuse;
They told the fairies to desist
And then they called a truce.

Sir John was very chastened
By all that had occurred,
And freely said he must have seemed
A creature most absurd

For all the silly things he'd done.
He said, 'I've been so crass,
And I begin to see at last
I've acted like an ass.

'I am at your disposal
And so will thus fulfil
Whatever things you wish of me –
Please use me as you will.'

At this they all laughed heartily –
Page, who was standing there,
Said, 'Let's go back to my abode
Where all of us can share

'A bottle of my finest sack.'
Jack Falstaff's eyes lit up.
He said, 'And will there also be
A chance for us to sup?'

Page laughed out loudly once again –
This was so like old Jack –
And then with glee he merrily
Clapped him across his back.

He said, 'And while you're at my house
There's one more thing you'll do,
For you can laugh there at my wife
Who right now laughs at you!'

Pericles, the Prince of Tyre
Found something out one day

PERICLES, PRINCE OF TYRE

Pericles, the Prince of Tyre
Found something out one day
That gave him such an awful shock
He had to run away.

The secret he unearthed about
Antioch's great King
Was something really terrible,
A vile and monstrous thing.

Whatever in the world was it
That caused the Prince to run?
What dreadful thing had happened?
What had this bad King done?

Well – he possessed a daughter,
A lovely-looking girl;
She set the heart of everyone
Aflame and in a whirl.

Her beauty brought her suitors
From far and wide, and so
One day the youthful Pericles
Thought he would have a go

To win the beauty for himself –
She'd make a lovely wife.
He knew, however, if he failed
Then he would lose his life.

Antiochus had set things up
In quite a cunning way,
And everyone who failed found out
There was a price to pay.

To win his precious daughter's hand
A riddle must be solved.
Those who failed would meet their death,
No-one would be absolved.

But Pericles thought, 'I must try',
For she was quite a catch,
And everyone at court all thought
They'd make a lovely match.

So off he went to see the King
And meet his daughter too,
For he was quite determined
To see the project through.

They handed him the riddle...
'Solve it,' the vile King said,
'And you, my dear Prince Pericles,
Shall share my daughter's bed.'

So Pericles perused the words
And to his horror saw
That they concealed a wicked act
That was against the law.

Other suitors hadn't twigged
But Pericles, in a flash,
Discerned the meaning and it turned
His every hope to ash.

For though the riddle tried to hide
The answer – not impart
The very deed that it contained –
This wise Prince, with a start,

Perceived that in it was revealed
Admission to a fact
That decent people all abhor,
A really awful act.

The King had practised incest
With his young daughter there;
The whole affair was obvious,
They were a brazen pair.

The young Prince was astounded,
His feelings ran amok!
He did his best to cover up
His horror and his shock.

So when he gave his answer
He spoke thus to disguise
The fact he'd worked the whole thing out –
He told a few white lies.

But King Antiochus could see
That this good-looking youth
Had in a moment understood
The foul and tawdry truth.

'He's worked it out,' he whispered,
'But I'll play with him awhile.
Please take more time to answer,'
He said with artful smile.

Pericles was much relieved
To gain a short respite,
For he'd been worried for his life
As truthfully he might.

He decided there and then
That he would have to flee.
'I'm getting out of here,' he thought,
'Before he murders me.'

And so he rushed off back to Tyre,
And on arriving there
He said to Helicanus:
'We all must need beware.

'Antiochus sleeps with his girl
And so I fear that Tyre
Will feel the wrath of this bad King –
We'll all be in the mire,

'For he's aware, I know full well,
That I have worked it out.'
He then told Helicanus
What it was all about.

Helicanus up and spoke.
He said, 'I've known you since
You were a boy – so heed me well:
You now must flee, my Prince.

'Sail for Tarsus right away;
You must get out of here.'
Said Pericles, 'I think you're right.
I must leave home, I fear.'

And so he sailed for Tarsus
Just in the nick of time.
The King of Antioch was keen
To cover up his crime,

So sent his servant, Thaliard,
To murder Pericles.
But the Prince had sailed away...
He'd caught the evening breeze.

When he arrived in Tarsus
He found a famine there;
The city was in dire distress,
With hunger everywhere.

But Pericles saw he could help
By sharing out his food.
This put the Governor, Cleon,
Into a gracious mood.

'Thank you for your generous help,
Thank you for the bread,
And all the other tasty things,'
The grateful Cleon said.

And then from Helicanus
The Prince received a note.
It counselled him to watch his back
And this is what he wrote:

'Antiochus has been informed,
He knows just where you stay.
Before he sends assassins
You should hurry on your way.'

Once more with trepidation
Our hero, Pericles,
Takes ship and sets his sovereign course
Across the wine-dark seas.

But then a tempest seized the ship;
It tossed the craft around
Until it gave up fighting
And sank without a sound.

Everybody perished,
Except Prince Pericles;
He was washed up on a shore
Beneath some tall palm trees.

He walked along the lonely beach
And met some fishermen.
These lads were very kind to him
And gave him all the gen

About the land to which he'd come –
Pentapolis its name –
Simonides was ruler there
And he enjoyed great fame

For being good and kind and fair –
He'd never told a lie;
All called him 'good' Simonides –
He was a decent guy.

His daughter was called Thaisa,
Perfect in every way,
And celebrations were arranged
Upon the following day

To mark this daughter's birthday,
And tournaments would be
Fought by knights and princes
At court for all to see.

The Prince was keen to join the jousts
But had no gear to wear –
His armour had been lost at sea.
He felt a great despair.

He would have loved to join the fun
But he was in a hole,
For with no armour he could not
Assume an active role.

But then a fisherman came up
And said, 'Look what I've caught.'
It was the armour he had lost,
The very suit he sought.

And so next day he made his way
To court, so he could fight
With every brave, heroic prince,
And every valiant knight

Who strove to gain the honour
Of lovely Thaisa's praise,
By daring deeds of bravery
To make her passions blaze.

Bold Pericles fought very well,
He was a raging sight,
In fact his courage was so great
That he won every fight.

He made the knights and princes there
Look like they'd lost the plot,
And by the end of that fine day
He'd finished off the lot.

Thaisa was quite overcome
And so with trembling knees,
Bestowed her royal favour
On brave young Pericles.

In his triumphant moment,
The Prince felt Cupid's dart,
And to the lovely Thaisa
Completely lost his heart.

The Princess too was smitten
By this bold, handsome lad,
So when he asked to marry her
She turned to her old dad

With looks that very clearly told
Her father, she was hooked –
And with no more discussion
A wedding day was booked.

But Pericles was still afraid
Of Antioch's foul King,
So he did not divulge his rank;
He didn't say a thing.

Some months passed and then news came
Antiochus was now dead,
So Pericles told Thaisa,
'It is a Prince you've wed.'

Simonides was overjoyed;
He got in quite a state.
'My daughter's married to a Prince –
Well, this is really great.'

Helicanus had sent news;
He'd said, 'Come right away,
'Twould not be wise, my dear, young Prince,
To tarry or delay.

'Your subjects are impatient,
They want your presence here;
If you do not return at once
There could be grief, I fear.'

'I must go,' said Pericles –
Thaisa was with child,
So added, 'You remain right here,
The sea can be so wild,

'It would not be advisable
For you to make the trip;
We do not want you giving birth
While you're on board a ship.'

Thaisa wouldn't have it.
She said, 'I'll be OK.'
So Pericles agreed because
She always got her way.

And they set sail – but in no time
The skies began to rain,
And then a mighty storm ensued –
Such rotten luck again.

Thaisa shook with awful fear
For all that she was worth,
And then right there within the storm
The poor scared girl gave birth.

Her nurse caught up the baby,
And, as the infant cried,
Upon that tossing, storm-wracked ship,
Princess Thaisa died.

The nurse then took the baby girl
To Pericles and said,
'Here is your little girl, my Lord,
Your dear wife, though, is dead.'

Pericles was overcome
With dreadful pain and grief.
However much he cried and railed
It gave him no relief.

And he cried out above the storm,
'Ye Gods! Why do you give
Such goodly gifts to mortals
And then not let them live.'

He took the baby girl and said,
'May your sweet life be mild,
For no child ever had a birth
More blustery or wild,

'For you have lost the person
More dear than any other:
I have lost a loving wife,
And you a darling mother.'

The storm gave not the slightest sign
Of going to abate,
And a corpse on board a ship
Is something sailors hate.

For they were superstitious,
They felt they'd get no peace
And if the body stayed on board
The storm would never cease.

They came to Pericles and said,
'We must demand, my Lord,
The corpse of your departed wife
Be thrown now overboard.

'It is the only way by which
The weather will transform;
It is the only way to stop
This monumental storm.'

Pericles was well aware
Their fears were quite unfounded,
But if he argued, knew for sure,
That they would be astounded,

For superstition runs so deep
Within a sailor's creed –
Thus with sadness and remorse
Poor Pericles agreed.

He went to see his Thaisa
One last and final time;
He gazed down on her lovely face,
So peaceful and sublime.

He said, 'My dear, beloved wife,
I beg you pardon me,
For I've been told that I must cast
Your body in the sea.'

The sailors brought a casket,
And placed the girl inside;
And as they did it, Pericles
Stood by and softly cried.

He laid some precious gems within
The casket – then he wrote
A message saying who she was,
And lastly placed the note

Beside his wife just lying there –
The note conveyed a plea;
'If she is found, please bury her.' –
Then cast her in the sea.

Then when the storm abated,
The Prince said with a sigh,
'Unless we reach the nearest port
My child will also die.

'She needs good nursing right away,
The little babe is frail,
So plot your course with speed I say –
To Tarsus we will sail.'

Thaisa's chest was thrown about
In almost constant motion,
A fragile and a helpless thing
On that vast, mighty ocean.

It rose and fell and whirled about
Amid the deafening roar,
Until it was, by mighty waves,
Deposited on shore.

And as it lay upon the beach
It was discovered there
By servants who then carried it
To Cerimon, with care.

He was a great physician,
He really was the best,
And gingerly he opened up
Thaisa's burial chest.

And there he saw the Princess
With the jewels and the note –
The one you will remember
Her grieving husband wrote.

And then he looked upon her face,
Observing that her flesh
Did not seem dead and lifeless,
In fact it looked quite fresh.

Cerimon then scratched his head
And said, 'It seems to me
They acted very hastily
Who threw you in the sea.

'I think that there may be a chance
This girl is still alive;
I think with careful nurturing
That she may well revive.

'And though she looks as if she's dead
As she lies softly there,
I think that all she needs is warmth
And some refreshing air.'

And then just like a miracle,
Amid the servants' cries,
Thaisa started breathing –
She opened up her eyes.

She'd never actually been dead
But, by unhappy chance,
After giving birth had swooned
And gone into a trance.

'Wherever in the world am I?
What is this place?' she said.
Cerimon sought to explain
How all had thought her dead.

He showed the note that Pericles
Had written and then sighed,
'Everyone on board your ship
Believed that you had died.'

She read the note and then exclaimed,
In tones – oh, so forlorn,
'I have no recollection
Of my baby being born.

'And as I'll never ever see
My Pericles again,
I'll enter a religious house
And there I will remain.'

Said Cerimon, 'If that's your wish
Then take good heart, my dear;
The Temple of Diana
Is situated here.

'You can become a vestal
And in the temple share
A life of contemplation,
A life of pious prayer.'

And that is what sad Thaisa did,
Though missing Pericles:
She spent her time in fervent prayer,
Hands clasped, and on her knees.

Meanwhile despondent Pericles
Took back the little waif
To Tarsus and to Cleon
Where he thought that she'd be safe.

He spoke to Dionyza, who
Was friendly Cleon's wife:
'This is my child, Marina;
Her mother lost her life.'

He told them of the dreadful storm
And with paternal pride
Spoke of the babe Marina's birth
And how Thaisa died.

And then he said to Cleon
And Dionyza too,
'I cannot raise the child myself,
I don't know what to do.

'So can I leave her in your care?
For I would much prefer
She's raised within a family.
Will you look after her?'

Cleon and his wife replied,
'Of course we will, my Lord.
We will treat her as our own;
She shall be our ward.

'We owe you, Prince, so very much,
For all the food you gave,
You saved the whole of Tarsus from
A grim, untimely grave.

'So we will raise her properly
And if we need a spur,
The whole of Tarsus will ensure
We take good care of her.'

So having settled things this way,
And having thanked the pair,
Pericles returned to Tyre
And once more settled there.

Many years have now elapsed.
Marina has now grown
Into a daughter any man
Would gladly call his own.

She had the sweetest singing voice
And, oh, how she could dance!
In everything she did she had
The power to entrance.

Soft hair fell on her shoulders,
She had a lovely face,
And every action that she took
Was carried out with grace.

So maybe it is no surprise
She roused some jealousy;
Most came from Dionyza,
As we shall quickly see.

For Cleon's wife had given birth
About the self-same time
Thaisa bore Marina
In that inclement clime.

Their poor daughter was quite slow,
Perhaps because her days
Were spent beneath the shadow
Of Marina's constant praise.

Dionyza felt that if
Marina wasn't there
Her daughter would receive at once
Much more respect and care.

She wouldn't suffer every day
The gross indignity,
Of being made to feel that she
Was second best, you see.

She knew a very evil man,
One Leonine by name;
To have Marina murdered
Was Dionyza's aim.

But even wicked Leonine
Recoiled from such an act.
He said, 'She has such virtue –
All know this for a fact.'

'Then this is all more reason,'
Foul Dionyza said,
'Why the gods should have her,
Why she should be dead.'

Leonine spoke softly:
'It is my job to kill,
And so your faithful servant
Will go and do your will.'

And as he spoke Marina
Came walking by that way,
She was in mourning for her nurse
Who'd sadly died that day.

'Let Leonine go with you,'
Her jealous guardian sighed,
'For he is just as sad as you
That your poor nurse has died.'

Marina wished to be alone
And she at first resisted,
But Dionyza spoke again
And firmly she insisted.

So the two set off at once
And walked along the shore;
Marina had no inkling
Of what might lie in store.

But Leonine then up and said,
'My dear young lady fair,
I bid you now be silent
For you must say a prayer.'

'What do you mean?' Marina asked,
'Why have you brought me here?'
And then the poor girl realised
She had good cause to fear.

'Now say your prayer,' the man replied,
'There is no time to waste,
For I am sworn to do my work
Both cleanly and with haste.

'You do not need a lot of time
To pray – for what I hear
Is that the gods know everything
And they are quick of ear.'

'Do you intend to kill me?'
The hapless creature said.
'Why in the world should you require
To see this poor maid dead?'

'My mistress wills it,' he replied.
'I'm sorry you must die.'
'I've never caused offence,' she said.
'I've never hurt a fly.

'Why does she want to kill me?
Why ever must I bleed?'
He said, 'Mine's not to reason why
But just to do the deed.'

But at the very moment
That he drew out his knife
In awful preparation
To take the poor girl's life,

Pirates landed on the shore –
And, right before the eyes
Of Leonine, they carried off
Marina as their prize.

They took the girl to Mytilene
And on arriving there
They sold her to a brothel,
Much to her despair.

But she was most determined
That she would stay quite chaste,
And she was fiery in the way
She showed her great distaste.

*. . . they carried off
Marina as their prize*

So when the brothel owner
Sent clients to the maid,
She preached to them of virtue
In order to dissuade

These men from their intentions.
She made them feel ashamed –
And so they always went away,
Their passions duly tamed.

And then she even managed
To convert the brothel boss...
He wasn't very happy –
In fact he was quite cross,

But he saw there was no way
That he would stand a chance
Of changing her – so he agreed
She could teach song and dance

And show the others how to weave
And also how to sew;
And thus she kept her honour
Intact and all a-glow.

Back in Tyre, Prince Pericles
Decided he would go
To Tarsus – for he thought it time
For him to get to know

His daughter, whom he'd sadly left
So many years before.
He was most anxious now to see
His little girl once more.

When he arrived he heard the news
His daughter was now dead.
'We put up this fine monument,'
Sly Dionyza said.

She really thought she told the truth –
She *thought* the girl had died,
For Leonine had told her this,
But then, of course, he'd lied.

Poor Pericles was mortified.
With tears and trembling lip,
He rushed away from Cleon's court
And went aboard his ship,

Set sail at once and in good time
Arrived in Mytilene,
Which, of course, is where we know
Marina to have been.

The Governor of Mytilene
Put on his Sunday best,
Then boarding his official barge
Went out to greet his guest.

But when he said, 'I'm here to greet
This visitor who's come...'
Lord Helicanus sadly said,
'My master's very glum.

'He will not speak to anyone –
Let me make it brief:
He's lost his wife and daughter so
He's quite consumed with grief.'

The Governor, Lysimachus,
Said, 'I've a little plan –
A way, I think, that we could help
To brighten up this man.'

He thought that sweet Marina
Could really help a lot;
He was her fan and in his heart
He held a loving spot.

And so he sent Marina,
Although still very young,
To talk to this Prince Pericles,
For she was sweet of tongue.

If anyone could cheer him up
He thought Marina could,
For she was known by everyone
To be extremely good.

She went to see poor Pericles
And when he heard her speak
He sat up slightly in his chair –
Things did not look so bleak.

Then when he saw the girl's sweet face,
He thought, 'Upon my life,
She is the spitting image
Of my poor long-lost wife.'

He started asking questions.
'Tell me your tale,' he said.
Marina then began to tell
About the life she'd led.

She told him she was born at sea
And how her mother died,
How she was left at Tarsus –
Poor Pericles then cried.

For he now saw before him
His girl whom he'd been told
Was buried and forgotten,
Her body long since cold.

But here she was before him,
His little baby girl;
It made his mixed emotions
Erupt into a whirl.

He embraced his daughter;
Marina hugged him too.
He told her how he loved her –
She said, 'And I love you.'

But all of this excitement
Made Pericles feel strained;
I guess it's little wonder that
The poor man was quite drained.

He fell into a happy sleep
With many a heart-felt sigh,
And as he slept Marina
Sat lovingly close by.

And deep in sleep he had a dream
That he must go with haste
Unto Diana's Temple –
There was no time to waste.

When he arrived he should recount
The story of his life:
All his great misfortunes
And how he lost his wife.

When he arrived he should recount
The story of his life

So Pericles and his dear child
Made their weary way
Unto Diana's Temple,
Intending there to pray.

But, as they entered, standing there
Was Cerimon – the chap
Whose skill had raised poor Thaisa from
Her cold and deathlike nap.

And standing to one side of him
Was dearest Thaisa too,
And when she saw Prince Pericles
She absolutely knew

It was her long-lost husband.
She listened as he spoke,
And every word he uttered
Made poor Thaisa choke.

He spoke about his dear dead wife –
He broke down for a while –
Then spoke about Marina
And all about her trial.

Thaisa was quite overcome,
And she could bear no more.
She cried, 'Oh royal Pericles!'
Then fainted on the floor.

Pericles was most surprised,
He shouted, 'What's amiss?
Who is this fainting woman
And what means all of this?'

Cerimon addressed the Prince:
'Sir, listen well to me.
This poor lady is the one
You threw into the sea.

'You thought that on that dreadful day
Your wife had lost her life,
But I revived her with my skill –
This lady *is* your wife.'

Pericles was overjoyed
And with no further qualms
He said, 'Be buried once again
Within my loving arms.'

Pericles then told his wife,
'Here is your daughter fair.'
Thaisa was quite overcome
To see Marina there.

And then in front of everyone
The Prince said that he thought,
The Governor, Lysimachus,
And his dear girl should court.

They'd make a lovely couple,
And both the young folk said
They truly loved each other
And would be pleased to wed.

Now there is only one thing left
That it remains to tell:
Of Cleon and his wicked wife
And what to them befell.

The kindly folk of Tarsus, when
They learned of what they'd done,
Went wild with righteous anger
And all rose up as one.

They burned the royal palace –
And with nowhere else to hide
The desperate couple cowered
In their throne room, deep inside.

And there they died an awful death,
Alone, without a friend;
But you must know for all the rest
There was a happy end.

Pericles told Thaisa,
'Sadly your father's dead,
So thus in Pentapolis
We will now reign instead.

'And Lysimachus, must now take
Marina, his new bride
To Tyre and be the ruler there –
My daughter at his side.'

So these two noble heroes
Wore their respective crowns –
A satisfactory outcome
After all the ups and downs.

'Yes, I can do this kingly stuff'

KING JOHN

When Richard, King of England
Died on campaign in France,
His brother John was quick to say,
'I think this is my chance,

'To have a go at ruling too.
It's always been my hope
To be the King, for I believe
I've got the skill to cope.

'Yes, I can do this kingly stuff,
And I'll soon get the knack
Of reigning, but I'll make quite sure
To always watch my back.'

He never spoke a truer word
For trouble was in store,
Since Philip who was King of France
Was now hell-bent on war.

For he believed Prince Arthur,
A nephew of King John,
Was the one the English crown
Should be bestowed upon.

And who could say he wasn't right
For Arthur was the son
Of King John's older brother,
So he really was the one

To claim the throne of England –
But his hopes had come unstuck
When John had grabbed it for himself:
The Prince was out of luck.

Arthur at this time was young,
A mere lad in his teens,
Still being told to wash his ears
And eat up all his greens.

King Philip wanted him in charge,
Insisting he'd be glad
If Arthur was made England's King –
He really liked the lad.

But no surprise, that bad King John
Would not give up his throne
For some pubescent, pimply boy,
A child not fully grown.

An envoy from the French arrived:
'Philip's prepared to fight.'
King John responded: 'Hear me well –
Then get out of my sight.

'Tell Philip I'll fight war for war.'
His words came in a flood.
'And I will match him sword to sword,
And also blood for blood.'

The envoy thus addressed, replied,
'King John, you may be sure,
That Philip will not stand for this,
Your actions will mean war!

'For Arthur should be King by right,
He is the one to rule.'
King John replied, 'Tell Philip this –
Just stick to playing boule!

'Tell him to keep his nose right out
Of England's state affairs,
For if he interferes this way
He'll soon be saying prayers.

'For I'll give him a bloody nose,
One that I freely bet
He'll find extremely painful and
He will not soon forget.'

Queen Eleanor, King John's mama
Then had the final word,
She commented with solemn face
On all that had occurred.

She said, 'I blame that Constance,
Arthur's ambitious mum
For moaning to King Philip who
Has now become her chum.

'It's she who's got the French involved
And stirred events up thus.
She's the one who is to blame
For causing all this fuss.'

And so it was not long before
King Philip's men laid siege,
To Angiers, a town in France
Which owned as royal liege,

The King of England, now King John,
And every living soul
Within the town paid court to him;
It was in his control.

But Philip laid out his demands;
Said, 'Angiers, I vow
You'll come within the sphere of France,
You must surrender now.'

He told them very clearly,
'You have to do one thing,
And that is to accept right now
That Arthur be your King.'

And then he said, 'Once this is done,
And he's King of your town,
Well then I'll take the steps to give
Young Arthur, King John's crown.'

The citizens of Angiers
Would not accept this fate,
And so they cowered in the town
Behind their wooden gate.

But then an army came along,
Approaching from the west,
And it was led by bold King John
Beneath an English crest.

King Philip calmly tells King John,
'You must now step aside
And give your throne to Arthur here.'
'Get lost!' King John replied.

Philip addressed Angiers then
And said, 'You must now choose.'
But they knew well, what e'er they did
They only stood to lose.

And so both armies now surround
This town, so small and fair;
The passions of two countries
Combine and end up there.

Philip tells the citizens
Emotions all aflame,
'Arthur should be England's King.'
John makes his counter-claim.

'*I* am your King and Angiers
Is mine; I counsel you
That your allegiance is to me.'
What could the poor town do?

They said, 'We will surrender
To the King whose claim is true –
England's real and proper King.
So we say, "Which of you

'Is speaking to us truthfully?"'
Of course each one cried 'Me!'
So how could this be sorted out?
What would the answer be?

Well, no surprise, the armies fought –
But then both claimed they'd won.
Neither side was strong enough
That they could overrun

The other in the field, and so,
As it was getting late,
They had to give it up and own
To reaching a stalemate.

So then it was suggested,
Once they had called a halt,
That all this senseless bloodshed
Was entirely the fault

Of Angiers' poor citizens.
'It's down to them, the swine.
Now let's attack them as one force,
Let all our troops combine.'

When the townsfolk heard of this
They very quickly saw
They'd have to find a way to stop
The fighting and this war.

So they proposed a compromise.
'Let Blanche, King John's fair niece
Wed France's heir, the Dauphin,
And bring about a peace.'

And so it was agreed forthwith;
The pact was quickly made.
But there were many mortified
By this expedient trade.

For Arthur's mother, Constance, felt
That she had been betrayed.
She thought the French King was a fool –
A bad deal had been made.

For in the deal, King Philip gained
Control of much French soil,
But giving up her Arthur's claim
Made Constance's blood boil.

For in return King Philip vowed
He'd never now again
Push Arthur's right to England's crown,
In peace – King John could reign.

But then the papal legate
Arrived at court one day.
Pandulph was this fellow's name –
He had stern words to say.

Directing all his ire at John,
He spun things on their head;
With irritation in his tone
He turned to John and said,

'I do not like the man you've picked
To be the church's voice –
Canterbury's bishop there.
I do not like your choice.

'You should have asked me what I thought,
You really should have waited.
Change your mind or I will have
You excommunicated.'

John wouldn't take this lying down.
He had a fit of pique,
And said, 'Who does he think he is?
What an infernal cheek!'

And so he told the Cardinal,
'You haven't got a hope
Of getting me to do your wish.
Go tell that to the Pope.'

At this the Cardinal cried out,
'This is no papal whim.
I shall not tolerate this talk,
I'll have no truck with him.'

He excommunicated John;
He kicked him from the church.
And gleefully he smiled and said,
'That's knocked him off his perch.'

But John was not at all perturbed.
He just arranged a feast
And told his friends, 'I'll not be bossed
By an Italian priest.'

Then Pandulph made his way to France
And said to Philip there,
'If you don't break your pact with John,
Then you too should beware.

'I'll excommunicate you too
If you don't heed my plea.'
So Philip broke his truce with John
To please the papacy.

It's true that he was influenced
By the young Dauphin there,
Who told his father ruefully,
'I think you should beware.

'I feel you must give careful thought
To what would now be worse –
To lose proud England for a friend
Or suffer Rome's dread curse.'

So once again there is a war.
France and England fight,
To find out who will rule the roost,
Which King is in the right.

Young Arthur's fighting with the French
But, much to his dismay,
He's caught and John declares that he's
'A serpent in my way.'

And orders that the boy should die.
Hubert de Burgh is told
To take firm steps to make quite sure
The boy does not grow old...

In other words, to take his life –
It's pretty heavy stuff.
King John just wants poor Arthur dead;
He's really had enough.

But though the King has said with force,
'De Burgh, kill him today.'
Good Hubert just informed the King
He'd keep him out the way.

So for the moment Arthur lived
And though extremely scared,
He knew that for a while at least
His threatened life was spared.

But later, back in England
Where Arthur was in jail,
Hubert was ordered to perform
A deed that made him quail.

He's told to take young Arthur's sight.
Oh, such a ghastly thing –
Then murder him – the order comes
From John, poor England's King.

But Arthur pleaded to be spared
And Hubert changed his mind.
From being set to kill the boy
He turned to being kind.

For he was truly overcome
By this good, saintly boy
Whose life so far had not been blessed
With any real joy.

He said, 'You'll have to hide, my lad,
King John, he wants you dead.'
The poor boy thanked him but was still
Borne down with awful dread.

Then Hubert went to bad King John
And, telling lies, he swore
That he'd fulfilled the King's dear wish –
That Arthur lived no more.

King John was happy at this news,
But some Lords with him there
Now asked, 'How could you kill the lad?
How could you even dare?

But Arthur pleaded to be spared

'For royal blood runs through his veins;
He is your kith and kin.'
They told him he was guilty of
Committing mortal sin.

Unrest fermented in the land:
The people were on fire,
For hearing of poor Arthur's death
Filled them with rage and ire.

John called kind Hubert to him
And told him angrily,
'All this unrest is *your* fault,
It isn't down to me.

'For you're the one who killed that boy,
A young lad in his prime,
You're the rotten murderer
Who carried out this crime.'

What a cheek to lay the blame
Upon poor Hubert so!
The King had been the one to say,
'Hubert, you must go

'And kill young Arthur right away,
I want that young boy dead.'
'Do not despair – he's still alive,'
Then Hubert boldly said.

Just then bad news arrives that tells
How Arthur tried to flee,
But jumping from the castle wall
He failed to grab a tree,

And from that dizzy height he fell...
The Prince died there and then,
Leaving John the most despised
And hated of all men.

For everybody blamed the King.
They said, 'King John has spilled
Prince Arthur's noble, precious blood.
It's he who's had him killed.'

An army now invades from France
And many English Lords,
Join with the French against the King;
They pledge their English swords

To rid fair England of King John,
To throw him from his throne.
And now King John feels quite let down,
Abandoned – all alone.

So as the armies both prepare
To battle once again,
King John is feeling sick inside –
He's lost the will to reign.

He goes to Swinstead Abbey
And, once ensconced in there,
He is resolved to rest awhile...
Might even say a prayer.

But while he's there a monk decides
The King is just no good.
He walks around the Abbey grounds,
Face hidden by his hood,

And quietly makes up his mind,
Though with a heavy sigh,
It would be best for everyone
If England's King should die.

And so he poisoned bad King John

And so he poisoned bad King John –
But as he passed away
The English lords desert the French,
Come back on side that day.

And then another peace is made
As French troops all withdraw,
And once again we see the end
Of yet another war.

King John's young son, Prince Henry,
Who's quite a decent lad,
Says, 'Leave me now in peace awhile.
I want to bury Dad.'

And as we see King John's demise
There's just one other thing,
And that's to say, Prince Henry there
Became the English King.

And it was said at Henry's court:
'No-one, despite all ill,
Will ever conquer England's realm –
And no-one ever will.

'For England has no cause to fear –
Will have no cause to rue –
If England has a decent King
And to that King is true.'

And so they took advantage
Of the good and bounteous Lord

TIMON OF ATHENS

'It's lovely having money,'
Timon of Athens sighed,
'For I can spread my fortune
To friends both far and wide.

'And for the poorer folk as well
I do a lot of good.'
The trouble for Lord Timon was
That all the town's dead wood

Would come and ask his favour,
For they had all been told
He had a generous, giving way –
He had a heart of gold.

And so they took advantage
Of the good and bounteous Lord,
As did the whole of Athens
Who were of the same accord.

They knew he was the softest touch,
He could be put upon;
Without a doubt, he really was
An easy guy to con.

A painter with a picture who
Was looking for a sale
Would take it to Lord Timon's house
And tell him quite a tale

Of how he really valued
The good Lord's point of view –
How did he like the painting?
It's on the market too.

'Oh, is it really? What great news!'
Lord Timon then would say.
'How fortunate I've seen it now –
This is my lucky day.'

And with no hesitation,
Right there and in a flash,
He'd ask if he could buy it
And hand the man the cash.

Because he was the victim
Of every lying bluff
His house was crammed to bursting point
With loads of useless stuff.

And usually he also had
A lot of folk there too,
Each with a sad sob story –
Sometimes they'd form a queue.

For everyone was on the make:
Painters and poets too,
And lords and ladies after help –
Oh what a fine to-do!

They flattered daft Lord Timon,
And he, with happy grin,
Declared them all his dearest friends –
Completely taken in.

So let's home in on one such day
When good Lord Timon saw
A load of begging suitors
Arriving at his door.

Someone speaks up first and says,
'My Lord, will you give bail
For your good friend Ventidius
Who's in the debtor's jail?'

'With all my heart,' Timon replied,
And told the man to go
Straight to the jail to save his friend,
And gave a pile of dough.

Then an old man there requests
A dowry for his daughter,
He leads Lord Timon by the nose,
A lamb unto the slaughter.

He said, 'Your man, Lucilius,
Has fallen for the maid,
But as he has no money
Someone must give him aid.'

And once again Lord Timon dug
Deep in his pocket there.
Anyone who asked for help
Was sure to get a share.

He gave the town a banquet
And, as the feasting ends,
Lord Timon cried, 'Now gather round.
I count you all as friends.'

He threw a casket open wide
And there they saw displayed
A thousand of the finest gems
That man has ever made.

He means to spread them all around –
He finds it all great sport.
He doesn't know, however, that
His funds are running short.

His faithful servant, Flavius,
Is standing there aghast,
Because he knows his master's wealth
Has not got long to last.

And Apemantus, who was there,
A cynic to the core,
Was quite appalled and horrified
By everything he saw.

He said, 'These greedy people
Are like leeches in the mud;
I grieve to see so many dip
Their meat in one man's blood.

'I scorn the whole foul pack of them –
Scroungers one and all.
But most of all I grieve and dread
To think what might befall.'

Now Timon owed a senator
A tidy little sum;
He'd borrowed it to help him with
Some kindly deed he'd done.

But on the grapevine it was heard
A rumour, and it said:
'Lord Timon's funds are getting low,
He'll soon be in the red.'

The senator was not amused.
He said, 'I'll be bereft;
I'd better try and get mine back
While he's got something left.'

He sent his servant there and then
To get his money back,
But when the servant reached the house
He found an angry pack

Of people also on the hunt
To get their cash returned.
It seemed that Timon's wealth was gone,
From what the man discerned.

For everyone was crying out,
'Give us our money now!'
You've never heard such noise before –
They made an awful row.

When Timon realised at last
That he was short of cash,
The penny dropped, you might observe,
With an almighty splash –

He really was in trouble now,
He owed more than he had.
He called his servant, Flavius,
And blamed the poor young lad.

'Why did you let this happen?
Why was I not informed?'
He shouted and he screamed at him –
Oh, how Lord Timon stormed!

But then he thought: 'A man who gives,
A man who always lends,
Can, when in trouble, surely count
Upon his many friends.'

He sent his servants to his friends
With orders to persuade
These so-called 'friends' to send some help
And give financial aid.

But all without exception
Made excuses pretty weak.
One said, 'I'm short of funds right now,
My prospects look quite bleak.'

Another said, 'I have no time
To think of this today.'
One even said, 'I would have helped
If I'd been asked to pay

'Before you asked the other folk;
I really must tell you
I would have helped, if I'd not been
The last one in the queue!'

So Timon came up with a ruse
To pay them back in kind.
He told his friends, 'You're well aware
That I am in a bind.

'But please ignore that now and come
To banquet here tonight.'
They went with no-one caring
About the poor man's plight.

And once they were all seated
The dishes then were brought,
The guests thought they contained cooked meat
Or fish just freshly caught.

But when they were uncovered,
To everyone's surprise,
The gathered throng could not believe
What lay before their eyes:

The dishes held hot water –
Just that and nothing more.
The greedy company was shocked
By what they all then saw.

For Timon stood before them
With anger on his face,
And with tremendous force he yelled
'Begone, and leave my place.'

He threw the water at them

He threw the water at them,
The dishes there as well;
And in their haste to get away
Some tumbled down and fell.

'Get out, ungrateful curs!' he cried.
'Just get out of my sight!'
There was no doubt Lord Timon gave
Those present quite a fright.

But once they'd gone he bowed his head
And said, 'I'll hated be,
From this sad moment till the end,
By all humanity.

'I'm finished with the lot of them!
Good Timon is no more.
No-one will get a welcome now
By knocking at *my* door.'

Alcibiades, meanwhile,
A captain of the guard,
Is pleading with the senate
That they won't be so hard

In dealing with a soldier
Who is about to die:
He'd got into a fight and then
Had killed the other guy.

It seemed the sentence would be passed,
The man would be a goner,
Though Alcibiades declared
The fight was one of honour.

The senate wouldn't listen.
They said, 'The man's a lout,
A menace to society –
Of that we have no doubt.'

He argued and he pressed his case
Till they'd all had enough.
They said the senate wasn't there
To listen to such stuff.

'You're banned from Athens,' they announced.
'So get out right away.
Don't ever let us catch you here
On any future day.'

The furious Alcibiades
Then left with but one thought:
That he would get revenge and this
Was now the end he sought.

He'd lead a band of angry troops,
Of discontented men,
Against the city and take power –
And once he'd won he'd then

Exact revenge upon this gang
Of senators who'd said
That he was banished – he'd not rest
Till all of them were dead.

Lord Timon has left Athens;
He's turned his back on life.
Within his soul bleak thoughts of hate
Are now all running rife.

He's living in the forest,
Hating anyone he meets,
And roots are now the only thing
That poor Lord Timon eats.

A broken man, he lives this life,
A hermit on his own,
And, knowing how his friends were false,
Prefers to be alone.

But then one day while digging
He finds beneath a root
Something to change his way of life –
He finds a pile of loot.

It is the most amazing sight,
Beneath the dirt and mould:
A really quite enormous pot
Of sparkling, yellow gold.

A really quite enormous pot
Of sparkling, yellow gold

You'd think he'd cut his losses,
Go back to Athens town;
But no – the actions of his friends
Have really pushed him down.

He stays there in the forest,
Alone and out of sight,
And every action that he takes
Is carried out with spite.

For he recalled that it's been said
Gold has destructive power;
And so he vowed maliciously
That he'd spend every hour

Making the pot of gold he'd found
Do what it's meant to do:
'I'll make it cause despair and grief
Before I'm good and through.'

Then seeing Alcibiades
Walk the forest there,
He gave him lots of gold and said,
'Now please take every care

'To slaughter lots of people
Within old Athens town,
For it's way overdue for them
To get their just come-down.'

And then he gave the army's whores
Some cash and told them, 'Please,
Make all the soldiers sick with pox –
Infect them with disease.'

And then he met some bandits –
He gave them cash as well.
He said, 'The whole wide world's a thief.
It's not far short of hell.'

He said, 'Go off to Athens,
But not to get a job;
Once you are there I beg of you
To pillage and to rob.'

Oh, what a change of temperament!
What a vindictive soul!
To foster misery and strife
Was now his only goal.

But then his servant, Flavius,
Approached him in the wood.
He tries his best to comfort him
And make him once more good.

But Timon will have none of it.
He says, 'I can't recall
I ever had an honest friend –
They're spongers, one and all.

'No-one is ever loyal.
They want what they can get;
And you're the same as all of them –
Just after gold, I'll bet.'

Flavius did his best to show
He meant his master well,
The man was really mortified
To see his master dwell

Alone within the forest
In such a desperate state,
To find his once kind master
So overcome with hate.

Timon said, 'Here, have some gold.
It's what you came here for.
Take it now and then clear off,
And bother me no more.'

So Flavius with sadness left,
And going heard him say
These final words of hate and bile
To speed him on his way:

'Hate everybody that you know –
A curse on everyone.
And most of all I tell you this:
Show charity to none.'

And yet young Flavius returned,
Two senators with him,
They thought they'd try just one more time,
Although their chance seemed slim,

To turn Lord Timon's view around,
To plead for him to come
To Athens, where they're now afraid
They'll be attacked by scum.

They mean, of course, the army
That Alcibiades leads.
They try to tell poor Timon there
Of all their pressing needs.

'Come back to Athens,' they implore.
'Do not delay an hour.
And, once you're there, we beg of you
To take again your power,

'And help us fight this army
That even now grows near.'
And Timon, though in sorry state,
Could smell and feel their fear.

But he gives not the slightest toss;
He doesn't care at all
About the army at the gates
And all that might befall.

He says, 'I'm busy writing
My epitaph, you see;
For very soon you'll hear about
The tragic end of me.

'But I'll give you one final word
Of sound and good advice.'
When he spoke, it must be said,
It wasn't very nice.

He said, 'You're getting in a state,
Worked up and in a froth –
Well, here's a way you can escape
The coming army's wrath.'

And then he chuckled to himself
And slowly shook his head.
'I suggest that all of you
Go hang yourselves,' he said.

The senators then left him there –
Each wore a sombre frown –
And made their weary, tired way
Back home to Athens town.

And there with Alcibiades
They parleyed and they spoke –
Of course they were all hoping
He'd prove a decent bloke.

'Go hang yourselves,' he said

For they had then decided,
Before it was too late,
To call a truce and strike a deal
And open Athens gate.

The terms of Alcibiades
He claimed were quite minute,
Though some might say he acted like
A cold, blood-thirsty brute.

He said he wanted all his foes –
And Timon's foes as well –
To lose their lives – his words were like
An edict out of Hell.

But that's the way things were back then:
For getting war to stop
There always was a price to pay,
There had to be a sop.

But then they heard of Timon's death,
Which at that time occurred,
And with the news the message brought
Lord Timon's final word.

'Here lies Timon of Athens
Who's thrown off life's great weight,
Who when alive did here avow:
"All living men I hate." '

The bitterness was clear to see
By all who stood around,
They cast their eyes in sympathy
Down at the cold, dark ground.

Here was a man who'd striven to
Do good things in his time,
And disillusionment had been
The poor man's only crime.

The irony did not escape
The people there that day,
They knew that generosity
Had once been Timon's way.

He'd done a lot of good with gold;
He'd used his wealth to spread
Good will to everyone he knew –
But now his old friends said

He also used his wealth to breed
Discord and fear and hate,
And to encourage folk to fight
And get into a state.

It showed a moral lesson
That all men understood:
Wealth could be used for evil ends
Or as a force for good.

Then Alcibiades declared
He felt poor Timon's pain,
And in that moment vowed aloud
He'd not wage war again.

He gazed around the gathered throng,
And said, 'Let anger cease.
Let's all unite as brothers now,
And make our war breed peace.'

'For I would have some words with you
About my new decree'

LOVE'S LABOUR'S LOST

The young, bold King of great Navarre
Bade three Lords, 'Come to me,
For I would have some words with you
About my new decree.'

And so Berowne and Longaville,
And also Lord Dumaine,
Asked him, 'What do you wish of us?
Please make your meaning plain.'

The King replied, 'I would impose
Upon you three Lords here,
A duty that will do you good
For many a long year.

'For I intend to make Navarre
A centre of great learning,
And wish for knowledge – that alone –
To fill your every yearning.

'So now, my Lords, I ask you all
To join me in my quest;
And please don't look at me that way
For this is not a jest.

'For we will spend the next three years
In study and we'll keep
A strict régime of fasting and
Restrict our hours of sleep.

'And, most of all, we will suspend
All fraternising stuff
With ladies, and although you'll find
That this will be quite tough,

'It's crucial to this plan of mine
That women are denied.'
Two of the Lords there said, 'OK.'
But Lord Berowne just sighed,

And then, collecting all his thoughts,
He said, 'Beloved King,
This all sounds most commendable
But you forget one thing.

'For in this contract here you say
No woman can defile
Our firm resolve to live alone
Or come within a mile.

'Your court will be for men alone,
And we three will be blamed
If we are found with women fair –
You say we will be shamed.

'And, most of all, we will suspend
All fraternising stuff'

'Yet even as you ask this thing,
Exert your royal power,
As you implore it's for our good,
Right now, upon this hour,

'A Princess from fair France arrives –
She's coming here today;
Surely the Princess, once she's here
Blows all resolve away...

'For you should not converse with her.'
The King said, 'She comes here
Upon a business trip, and so
I must have words, I fear.'

Berowne then sighed and slowly said,
'Though I'm loathe to agree,
I'll sign and thus I do, my Lord,
Accept this new decree.'

Lord Boyet's with the French princess;
He gives advice and aid,
For though she is of royal blood
She still is but a maid.

He tells her, 'Please remember that
You've come here in the main
To talk about the status of
The land of Aquitaine.'

The Princess is accompanied
By three young ladies fair:
Rosaline and Katharine –
Maria too is there.

The ladies are all talking
About Navarre's great Lords,
What dashing men they seem to be
With capes and ruffs and swords.

The men are all so bold and brave
And handsome and so kind.
Now could it be that these three girls
Have romance on their mind?

Maria once saw Longaville
In Normandy one day.
'I think he is a fine, young man,'
The girl was heard to say.

And so she told the other two,
'There is no man to match
Lord Longaville – I'm sure he'd be
A really worthy catch.'

Then Katharine said, 'I do believe
That Lord Dumaine is nice.
He's noble, honest – oh so fine –
Quite free of any vice.'

Rosaline, on hearing this,
Said, 'I think best of all
Is Lord Berowne; he's so well built,
So muscular and tall.

'I spent an evening with him once –
He had me in a fit
With all his funny jokes and tales
And with his ready wit.'

And thus the young girls carried on
With these romantic tales
About their brief encounters with
These dashing, brave, young males.

But then the King himself comes in
And makes his way towards
The Princess and her ladies there
Attended by his Lords.

He says, 'I'm very sorry but
You can't stay with us gents.
I hope you'll be quite comfortable
Within these humble tents.'

The Princess had been told about
The King's three-year decree,
And though she didn't like the tent
She said, 'It's fine with me.'

She reads a letter from her Pa,
Who is the King of France,
And while she reads out loud, the King
Is in a love-filled trance.

She says, 'The Aquitaine belongs
To France.' And then she frowns.
The King replies, 'But what about
Our hundred thousand crowns?

'For that is what we're owed from France,
And once the sum is paid,
Why you can have the Aquitaine
And we'll complete the trade.'

The Princess says, 'You will receive
The proof we've paid quite soon;
In fact I think you should get word
Before tomorrow noon.'

But while all this was going on
It's no surprise to hear
The men had nobbled Lord Boyet,
To get the old chap's ear.

They asked him questions all at once
About the ladies there.
Dumaine said, 'Is there any chance
That Katharine might care?'

And Longaville said, 'I do think
Maria's quite sublime,
But tell me, sir, in honesty
If I do waste my time.'

Berowne then said of Rosaline,
'My Lord, she is the best,
But am I doomed to failure
In this, my lovelorn quest?'

Lord Boyet listened, while the fair
Princess and noble King
Discussed their business matters –
And he clearly saw one thing,

As if it were in words of fire,
As if it had been written:
The King was quite entranced, enthralled –
In fact, completely smitten.

And when the King had left that day
He made no great ado,
But told the Princess straight away,
'The King's in love with you.'

And so the four young gentlemen,
The nobles and their King,
Are deep in love, although they swore
They would not do this thing.

When each of them is safe away
From all the others' sight,
Each one sits down with pen and ink
And he begins to write.

For each has now turned poet and
Composes verses to
The lady who lights up his life,
To tell her, 'I love you'.

So they ignore their solemn vows –
What if the others find
That they have broken the decree,
Completely changed their mind?

Berowne, once finished, then commands
A servant, 'Take this note
To Rosaline, but make quite sure
It's tucked beneath your coat.'

He didn't want to take the chance
The others would find out.
They mustn't have an inkling
Of what he was about.

For truthfully, he was amazed
That love had struck him so –
That he was now resolved to be
Sweet Rosaline's own beau.

He mused a while and spoke these words,
'Never in my life
Would I have thought that I would love –
That I would seek a wife.

'But now I love, I sigh, I groan,
But most of all I pray
That Rosaline will take me as
Her husband, one fine day.'

Then later on Berowne climbs up
One of the royal trees
And makes himself a hiding place.
There, looking down, he sees

The King below, with poetry –
He's reading it out loud!
Its contents show he's thrown away
All that *he* has avowed.

The poem which the King declaims
Up to the heavens above
Is all about the French Princess
With whom he's now in love.

The King in turn hears Longaville
As he is reading too
A sonnet to Maria –
It's lovelorn through and through.

Then Longaville pricks up his ears –
It will be no surprise
That he now hears Dumaine proclaim
His love has such blue eyes.

The King below, with poetry

118

He was professing to the world
That Katharine, his love,
Was quite the fairest in the land,
His own beloved dove.

And thus it was that these three youths,
Each secretly, has heard,
The other breaking his strict vow,
Every fervent word.

And so they then admit the truth,
Each one of them in turn.
The King says, 'We're in trouble
If Berowne should ever learn,

'That we've so quickly thrown away
Our firm resolve and vow' –
But as he spoke Berowne himself
Descended from his bough.

He says, 'You each have been untrue
And chosen to ignore
The solemn oath that we all took –
Denied the vow we swore.'

They looked around shamefacedly
And each of them came clean.
Berowne then really rubbed it in,
How sneaky they had been.

But then his servant comes and says,
'I got into a mix;
The wrong note I gave Rosaline.'
Berowne was in a fix,

For as he spoke he handed him
The poem and he said,
'So here it is, unopened, sire.'
Berowne then turned bright red.

He grabbed the note and tore it up,
Then threw it on the ground.
Dumaine though picked the pieces up,
And then of course he found

Berowne had also been untrue
And thrown aside his vow.
The King declared, 'We're all as one.
So what should we do now?'

Turning to Berowne he said,
'You must now find a way
To prove our loving's lawful,
To show that it's OK.'

Berowne was nimble on his feet,
He had an agile mind,
And it would surely help him out
If he could quickly find

A way to justify the fact
That they had all denied,
The oath they solemnly had sworn –
For each of them had lied.

He glanced around at his dear friends,
At their expectant looks,
And said, 'Love teaches many things
That can't be found in books.

'And so I think that when we love
We also study too,
So following our heart's desire
Is quite the thing to do.'

And then they nodded sagely.
This seemed to justify
Their actions and to thus condone
Each lover's roving eye.

The King said, 'We will entertain
The ladies now we're set,
And with good luck – who knows? – we may
Gain their affections yet.'

Berowne said, 'Let the revels start...
We'll pass some merry hours.
Let true love run her tender course;
We'll strew her path with flowers.'

And so the King with his three Lords
Attends the ladies fair,
And they enjoy great revelry
And partying, once there.

But then a messenger arrives,
Which ruins fun and dance
Because he brings the gravest news
About the King of France.

The poor old King has passed away,
The monarch now is dead.
'Oh my beloved father, dear!'
His grieving daughter said.

The Princess must return at once
And, though borne down with pain,
She thanks Navarre for giving back
The much loved Aquitaine.

The men, on seeing they're to leave,
Swear to the heavens above
Their actions weren't just fun and games –
They then avow their love.

The Princess turned to face the King,
Upon her cheek one tear.
She said, 'I'll mourn my father now
Until this time next year.

'If in that time you will agree
To be just on your own,
Remote from pleasure and all fun,
And live your life alone,

'And if when this twelve-month has past
You still feel much the same,
Then I will be your loving wife;
I'll take, fair King, your name,

'And we will live as man and wife.'
Then, with no backward glance,
She climbed onto her horse at once
And rode right then for France.

The Lords too watched their ladies
Depart in the same way,
And they could only hope that they'd
Come back to them one day.

For they would have to wait the year,
Alone, what e'er the cost,
To find if they had won their love
Or were 'Love's Labour's Lost'.

*'I've never ever heard
Of such a cheeky thing'*

EDWARD THE THIRD

Our tale begins as Edward, King
Of England, makes the claim
That he should rule all France as well –
The French throne is his aim.

But it will come as no surprise
That John, who's France's King,
Declared, 'I've never ever heard
Of such a cheeky thing.'

He sent the good Duke of Lorraine
To Edward, there to say,
'You have no right to France and so
Just take your claim away.

'Instead, however, you can be
In France a senior Duke.'
King Edward up and answered him
With swift and stern rebuke.

'I soon shall come to France and take
Your kingdom – make it mine,
And then forever more it will
Be passed on down my line.'

But then King Edward's mind was turned
Onto another thing –
Which makes it very clear indeed
It's hard to be a king.

For David, King of Scotland,
Has flexed his regal might
And sent a force to England –
And they're prepared to fight.

As Edward there was thinking
Of France and what to do,
King David was besieging
A countess Edward knew.

She was at Roxsburgh castle
And things looked bad indeed.
She was desperate for help –
She had most pressing need.

King Edward said, 'The Countess
Of Salisbury is my friend,
I will not contemplate that she
Should meet a rotten end.

'So I will go to Roxsburgh
And punish all the Scots;
I'll finish off King David
And all his silly plots.'

Then turning to his much-loved son,
Prince Edward, who was known
As the Black Prince, he said to him,
'I trust to you alone

'The task to raise an army
And then I think, perchance,
Across the English Channel you
Should go, and capture France.'

With this all settled, Edward then
Set off that very day
For Roxsburgh, where he soon found out
The Scots had run away.

The countess said, 'My precious liege,
Thank goodness that you're here.'
The King replied, 'You're quite safe now.
There's nothing more to fear.'

He really should have chased the Scots
But he was in a whirl –
When he beheld the countess there
He sighed, 'My, what a girl!'

And though he was a married man
He vowed that he would do
A thing quite out of order:
He'd do his best to woo

The lovely countess whom he'd saved,
For surely she'd be glad
To gain attention from a king –
From such a likely lad.

He walked around enraptured,
He sighed and spoke of love,
He said the apple of his eye
Was really way above

All creatures in this mortal world –
That nothing could compare...
And if his love was not returned
He'd wither in despair.

He told his servant, Lodwick,
'I've really got the blues,
And so I want you now to write,
Inspired by your muse,

A poem that will stir the soul –
Her beauty fills my heart.'
'Is it a woman?' Lodwick asked,
As he prepared to start.

Edward cried, 'You fool! You knave!
It's for a lass, of course.
Oh, wretched man, did you believe
I'd bid thee praise a horse?'

Lodwick tried his best to write
A poem for the lass,
But in truth his every word
Was feeble, weak and crass.

So Edward grabbed the pen and wrote
Of love and pain and how
He loved the countess best of all,
That he must have her now!

But then the countess sashayed in,
She waltzed into the room,
And seeing Edward's mournful face
Said, 'Why, my Lord, such gloom?

'You look fed up and so morose,
Pray tell me, Highness dear,
If there is something I can do
To make that deep frown clear.'

Sneaky Edward saw his chance.
He thought, 'I'll tell her how
To cheer me up, but first of all
I'll make her take a vow.

'Now will you promise me you'll cure
This sad, unhappy man?'
The countess said, 'Of course I will.
I'll do the best I can.'

'Then be my mistress,' Edward cried.
'To love you is my goal.'
She cried, 'If I submit to you
I'll sacrifice my soul.

'I owe my husband faithfulness
As you owe to your queen;
To take you as my lover
Would be most base and mean.'

The King replied, 'You promised me
You would do all you could
To make me happy, so I thought
You clearly understood

'That it was all agreed and set –
You'd honour this your vow;
So I demand that you fulfil
Your solemn promise now.'

But still the countess wouldn't budge,
So Edward, sly and bad,
Approached the Earl of Warwick,
Who was the lady's dad.

He said, 'Instruct your daughter
To be my mistress now.'
The Earl reluctantly agreed
And with a sweeping bow

He left the room, and made his way
To his poor daughter fair.
He said, 'You can't refuse the King –
You'd be a fool to dare.

'It's best to lose your honour,
Not sacrifice your life.'
She cried, 'I have a husband
And King Edward has a wife.

'If I'm his mistress I betray
My loving husband's trust,
So I refuse to be a toy
For Edward's graceless lust.'

The Earl of Warwick was relieved –
His girl had proved to be
A fine, upstanding, moral wife.
He said, 'I'm pleased to see

'That you are so determined
To tell the King to go
And seek a mistress somewhere else –
That you don't want to know.'

And so, returning to the King,
They both walked through the door.
He looked up hopefully and said,
'So tell me, what's the score?'

The countess said, 'I'll give to you
All that which you desire.'
The King looked up with lustful gaze –
His passions were on fire.

'But first we must remove those things
That stand there in the way
Of this our love – for my dear Lord,
There is a price to pay.'

The King looked at her quizzically –
What schemes were in her head?
'So what must we remove, my dear?'
He very softly said.

Without a word the countess then
Produced two long, sharp knives
And said, 'Between our love the thing
That stands is our own lives.

'Our deaths must come before our love.'
She offered him a knife.
Edward recoiled but she declared,
'I'll surely take my life

'Unless you promise here and now
Never to try again,
To have me for your mistress, sire,
For it is quite insane.'

Without a word the countess then
Produced two long, sharp knives

At this the King perceived that his
Behaviour had been bad;
He saw he'd been a lustful fool,
A bounder and a cad.

He promised from that moment
He'd show his lust the door,
And treat her as an English rose
Henceforth – and evermore.

Then Edward made his way to France
To join the Black Prince there,
And met with France's reigning King
And to him did declare,

'I've come to France to stake my claim
And ere the sun goes down,
I urge you step aside and give
This rightful King the crown.'

King John exclaimed, 'Pernicious wretch!
You foreigner! You swine!
I am the rightful King of France.
This kingdom is all mine.'

With all negotiations thus
Completely broken down,
Two armies there at Crecy field
Would battle for the crown.

And to the death they both would fight
To ascertain who'd own
The fair and favoured realm of France,
Who'd win the great French throne.

Before the battle, Edward called
His brave son to his side;
He gazed at him admiringly
And with a father's pride.

He said, 'As you prepare to go
To fight on Crecy field,
It is my solemn duty
To give you your first shield,

'A suit of shining armour,
A helmet and a lance;
Also a father's blessing, son –
Now win for me fair France.'

Prince Edward rode to battle,
Completely free of fears;
His father's final, loving words
Were ringing in his ears.

'You must earn your knighthood,
True honour must be won
In bloody, fearless fighting –
It's the only way, my son.'

And as the dreadful battle raged
His father's words rang true –
Prince Edward there was fighting,
And how his courage grew.

But word is brought unto the King:
'We fear for your son's life.
He's in the thick of battle,
Deep in the fray and strife.

'Shall we rescue him, my Lord,
Before it is too late?'
Edward just replied, 'No, don't.
We'll all stay here and wait.

'For I have other sons, you know,
To comfort my old age,
And he must earn his spurs today
Upon this bloody stage.

'This is his chance to season
His courage and his might.
He'll either die today or earn
The right to be a knight.'

136

Harsh words indeed, but then the King
Knew 'twas the only way
His son and heir could thus become
An honoured man that day.

And so it was that later on
Prince Edward came and said,
'A victory we here have won,
For all the French have fled.'

And then the King had more good news,
For he received the word
That yet another victory
Had recently occurred.

King David had been captured,
The Scots were on the run,
And so King Edward's forces
On two bold fronts had won.

But still he must remain in France –
The French weren't finished yet;
They still could field sufficient force
To be a serious threat.

The Black Prince now, once more prepares
To face the French again.
He's told they've gathered a huge force
On Poitier's great plain.

Lord Audley says, 'My royal Prince,
We face a mighty test.'
But Edward laughs and clearly shows
That he's quite unimpressed.

And then a messenger arrives,
And to the Prince does tender
A missive from King John that says,
'Be sensible – surrender!'

Again the Black Prince laughs and says,
'What an infernal cheek.
You tell King John, I do intend
To give his nose a tweak.'

Another message then arrives,
It comes from King John's son,
It offers Edward a fast horse
On which the Prince can run.

And then a little gift arrives,
It's brought to Edward there,
A present from the French – it is
A holy book of prayer.

The inference is very clear –
'Black Prince – get on your knees,
And pray the good Lord up above
Gives notice to your pleas.'

Prince Edward merely scoffs and says,
'Remove this from my sight.'
And then he pulls his visor down
And so prepares to fight.

The battle starts and at one point
King Edward's told for sure,
The Black Prince has been wounded
And that he lives no more.

He says, and others tremble as
They hear their monarch speak,
'If he is killed, such vengeance I
Will very surely wreak.

'For the Prince's funeral knell,
If I find out he's dead,
Will be the piteous cries and moans
Of dying men,' he said.

But as he speaks a trumpet sounds;
Prince Edward then strides in.
He's bloodied and bedraggled but
He wears a buoyant grin.

King John is now his prisoner –
He stands there looking down;
Prince Edward then triumphantly
Displays the French king's crown.

Prince Edward then triumphantly
Displays the French king's crown

He hands it to his father;
Then, standing proud and tall,
He shouts aloud to everyone,
'I tell you, one and all,

'I'll fight those French guys any time,
And Spain and Turkey too,
And anyone who wants a fight,
Well, they can join the queue.'

Elated now with victory,
Success set him on fire.
He cried, 'I'll fight all those who dare
Provoke fair England's ire.'

King Edward calmly shook his head.
'Patience, my son,' he sighed.
'It's time to rest, for I believe
Too many men have died.

'And so I say, don't fret and fuss,
Don't fume and froth and foam.
It's time we sailed for England,
It's time that we went home.'

'You are a cheeky servant boy'

THE COMEDY OF ERRORS

There long had been a quarrel
Between two famous states;
There was no way the two of them
Would ever be good mates.

Syracuse and Ephesus
Were how these states were called;
Their quarrel would make any man
Be really quite appalled,

For Ephesus had passed a law
Which made it very plain
That anyone from Syracuse
Would just be caught and slain

If they were found in Ephesus –
It's what the law decreed,
And there was only one sure way
The person could be freed.

That was by handing over
A load of ready dough;
A thousand marks was the set sum
To let intruders go.

It really was an awful law,
And what amazing cheek!
A way of making piles of cash
And bullying the meek.

It chanced one day a merchant,
From Syracuse, of course,
Was found to be in Ephesus –
They dragged him from his horse.

This poor old man was Egeon –
A crowd of rough, coarse men
With violent hands laid hold of him
And took him there and then

To see the Duke of Ephesus.
They cried out with a sneer,
'Look here, great Duke, upon this wretch,
Just see what we've got here.'

These common folk loved all such sport,
How they enjoyed these larks.
'Come on, you low-down merchant man,
We want a thousand marks!

'Or by the law you'll surely die.
Hand over cash, you swine.'
But there was just no way that he
Could ever pay the fine.

The Duke said Egeon must pay
Or else he'd have to die.
'But ere you do, you must relate,
You really must tell why

'You travelled here to Ephesus –
A stupid thing to do.
You knew if you were captured here
'Twould mean the end of you.'

Egeon sighed a weary sigh;
He said, 'My life's been tough,
And I don't care if I'm to die
For I have had enough.

'You tell me to recount my life,
The worst thing you could ask;
Reliving all my sorry woes
Is not a pleasant task.'

So then Egeon told his tale.
He said, 'It may amuse,
And while away some time for you –
It starts in Syracuse.

'For there it was that I was born.
A merchant I became;
I earned a decent living there
And a respected name.

'But then one day while on a trip
To Epidamnum town,
My wife gave birth to two fine boys,
Just as the sun went down.

'But in the golden evening light,'
Distraught Egeon sighed,
'On looking at my new-born sons
I suddenly espied

'That they were like each other
In infinite degrees;
So much, in truth, it's fair to say
They looked just like two peas.

'You couldn't tell the boys apart
One infant from his brother,
They lay there sleeping in their crib
And each looked like the other.

'But then the most amazing thing
Of which you've ever heard:
Within an hour of their birth,
Right there and then occurred

'The birth of two more lovely boys.
I swear to you by God,
That these infants also looked
Like two peas in a pod.

'Their mother and her husband
Were poor as poor could be,
And so I said, "I tell you what,
Give your two boys to me.

' "They can become the servants
To my two children here;
I'll see your boys are cared for well...
I pray be of good cheer,

' "For here is money that will help
The pair of you get through."
And so the deal was done right there –
It seemed the thing to do.

'They took the money gratefully,
So glad that they had found
A decent home for their two lads
And earned themselves a pound.

'And so our life went on until
My wife spoke out one day:
"I'm tired of Epidamnum.
Can we go home, I pray?"

'I didn't really want to go
But said we'd make the trip,
So we set sail for Syracuse
Next day aboard a ship.

'But shortly after setting sail
Black clouds began to form,
And we were caught inside an hour
Within a mighty storm.

'The sailors all saw straightaway
The ship could not survive,
There was alone one strategy
To keep them all alive.

'And that was to escape the ship
They knew would surely sink –
So that is what the cowards did,
Right then, within a wink.

'They launched the boats and all climbed in,
They left me there on board
With my dear wife and all the boys –
That is the truth, my Lord.'

The Duke was nodding gravely.
'What happened then?' he said.
'How in the world did you escape?
By rights you should be dead.'

'You speak the truth, my gracious Lord,
But when the going's rough
It heightens your resolve and will –
I guess it makes you tough.

'I tied my younger son right then
Unto a broken mast,
Likewise the younger servant boy,
And told them to hold fast.

'And then I bade my desperate wife
To do the same as well
With both the other lads – then we
Jumped in that foaming hell.

'We watched the stricken ship drive on
And break upon a rock,
At once within that raging storm
Our mast was thrown amok.

'And then with an almighty noise
The great mast broke in two;
My wife and both the older boys
Quite disappeared from view.

'The frightened younger lads and I,
Upon that ocean vast,
Just clung on tightly for our lives
To our poor piece of mast.

'Like matchsticks we were thrown around
All through the rain-lashed night,
But then I glimpsed my poor dear wife –
'Twas just a glancing sight.

We watched the stricken ship drive on
And break upon a rock

'A fishing boat was saving them –
I thanked the Heavens' Lord,
For I believed they were quite safe
As they were pulled on board.

'And then a mighty, crashing wave
Carried the boys and me
Away into the storm-filled night,
Across the inky sea.

'I fought against the angry waves,
Did everything I could
To save those boys there in my charge –
I clung on to the wood.

'And then, as with my wife before,
A fishing boat appeared,
And, happily, they snatched us from
The death which I had feared.

'They took us back to Syracuse,
All through that sea, so wild,
And since that day I've never heard
Of wife nor eldest child.

'My younger son grew curious,
When later he was told
Of what had happened on that night –
At eighteen he was bold –

'He said, "I'll go and search for them,
They must be somewhere, Dad."
Now how could I refuse his wish!
He's a persuasive lad.

'And so I finally agreed
To what he wished to do,
Yet with a quaking in my heart
That I might lose him too.

'But then I hoped he'd find my wife,
And end my wretched tears;
I thought that he might find her though
She had been lost for years.

'So off he went and took with him
His youthful serving lad...
I freely do admit to you
Their going made me sad.

'And then my very direst fears
Unhappily came true,
For it is seven years till now
Since my boy said "Adieu".

'And for the last five of these years
I've had but little peace,
For I have searched for him and been
As far afield as Greece.

'And finally I ended here,
For though it meant great danger
I hoped that I might be ignored
Although I was a stranger.

'I knew I risked great peril
By ever coming here,
But hoping I would find my son
I overcame my fear.

'And now the worst has happened
And I shall lose my life,
But I would die a happy man
If I could see my wife.'

The Duke was moved by all of this,
By all he heard and saw.
He said, 'I'd spare you if I could
But I can't change the law.

'But you shall have a further day
So you can have a bash
At borrowing or begging
A thousand marks of cash.'

Poor Egeon! He sighed aloud,
Despair across his face –
Whatever was the point of this
Unlooked-for day of grace.

He knew no-one in Ephesus;
It just delayed his end,
For in that place he did not hope
To find a single friend.

But hold a moment, for right there
In that unfriendly town
Were people who could soon dispel
Sad, old Egeon's frown.

For at that time in Ephesus
There dwelt the very ones
For whom he sought so fervently –
Yes, his beloved sons.

The older son had lived right there
For twenty years or more;
The younger had arrived that day,
Despite the town's cruel law.

These lads had both the self-same name.
Confusing? – Yes, I know.
Both were called Antipholus.
A nuisance – yes … and so,

To tell them both apart we must
Apply this simple ruse:
The younger son, Antipholus,
Will be 'of Syracuse'.

And to the older of the twins,
We now assign the name,
Antipholus of Ephesus –
Just treat it as a game!

But it gets more confusing still
As both lads had close by
The servants whom their dad had bought...
Now this will make you sigh –

For *they* both have the self-same name,
Exactly as the other:
Each one was known as Dromio,
The same as his twin brother.

Thus one of them is Dromio
Of Ephesus, and so
The other is 'of Syracuse' –
And now this fact you know.

To make the story easier,
To make the rhythm flow,
We shall devise a little ruse:
Here it is – and so

Antipholus of Syracuse
Becomes Antipholus S,
We'll give his man an S as well,
And this should ease the mess.

And thus, of course, Antipholus
Of Ephesus will be,
Along with servant Dromio,
Attended by an E.

So back now to our story.
As I've already told,
Antipholus E had lived right there –
And he was rich and bold.

For he had been befriended
By the Duke some years before;
He'd been a soldier and had then
Shown bravery in war.

And so the Duke, as just reward,
('For all you've done' he'd said),
Betrothed him to a lovely lass
And so the pair had wed.

This lady, Adriana,
Was rich and also fair –
And he was living in this way
When his old dad came there.

Also with this Antipholus
Was someone else we know:
His faithful servant and good friend,
The young lad, Dromio.

But in another part of town
We find the second twin.
Antipholus S has just arrived,
Close to his other kin.

That he had come from Syracuse
Meant he should watch his back –
A friend there lets him know just how
He can avoid all flak.

'Say you're from Epidamnum,'
The crafty friend had said.
'For if you don't, you may well find
You quickly end up dead.

'An old guy out of Syracuse
Was caught sometime today,
And he's about to lose his life
Because he cannot pay

'The thousand marks the Duke requires –
It's really very sad.'
Antipholus S had no idea
The friend spoke of his dad.

Antipholus then straightway sent
Young Dromio S to find
An inn where they could spend the night,
Where they could both unwind.

Whilst Dromio S went looking
He walked around some more,
But glancing up he was surprised
At what he thought he saw.

For Dromio S was coming back –
Already – in a tick;
Surely he'd not booked the inn...
How had he been so quick?

But this was Dromio E, to whom
Antipholus S then said,
'Why are you back so quickly?'
Dromio shook his head.

He said, 'My mistress bids you come
To dinner right away.'
'What mistress?' asked Antipholus.
'Who is this lady, pray?'

'Why, your dear wife,' the lad replied.
Antipholus lost his cool.
'I do not have a wife,' he said.
'Why do you play the fool?'

Dromio E thought this just fun
And told him once again
That dinner was awaiting him –
He made his plea in vain.

Antipholus S then beat him
And said, 'Upon my life,
You are a cheeky servant boy
For I don't have a wife.'

Dromio E then ran off home.
When Adriana heard
Her husband had denied her thus
And all that had occurred,

She fell into a jealous rage.
Her spouse had ceased to care.
What in the world was going on?
'He's having an affair!'

She found out where her 'husband' was,
And where the poor man stayed,
And off she went with all due haste –
She was an angry maid.

And on arriving there she found
Antipholus S, of course;
She thought the showdown that would come
Might well lead to divorce.

For she was quite determined
That she would gain the truth,
So when she found him there, she yelled –
The poor man just cried, ''Strewth!'

'You've been untrue to me'

He didn't have an inkling
Who this strange lass could be.
She cried, 'You've got another love.
You've been untrue to me.'

He said he didn't know her
But she replied to this,
'You are my husband, my true love.'
And tried to plant a kiss.

At last she said, 'Come home, at once,
My husband – I insist.'
Antipholus S could see no way
To anymore resist.

He went then to his brother's house
And there sat down to dine
With his dear 'wife' – her sister too –
They had fine food and wine.

Dromio S had come as well
And found his way into
The kitchen, where the female cook
Just stuck to him like glue.

She said she was his own dear wife –
So more confusion here –
But even greater trouble now
Was swiftly drawing near.

Antipholus E approached the house,
Returning home to eat,
But when he knocks upon his door
His servants there entreat,

'Be gone at once, good sir, because
Our mistress has made clear
She's dining with her husband now.'
He cried, 'What's that I hear?'

He yelled and remonstrated,
He yelled and yelled some more,
But these obedient servants
Wouldn't let him through the door.

Finally he went away,
A most unhappy soul –
To find out what was going on
Had now become his goal.

Antipholus S, a puzzled man,
Is finishing his meal –
He's sick of Adriana
And all her crazy spiel,

So he is keen to get away;
He puts down fork and knife,
Preparing his excuses now
To leave this cranky wife.

He doesn't like her very much.
Her sister, who's there too –
Well, she's a different matter,
And he takes a different view.

The truth is that he fancies her
But that will have to wait,
Though he's determined at some time
He'll try to get a date.

Luciana was the sister
And, despite her being there,
He apologised for going
And got up from his chair.

'I really must be on my way,
So thank you for the food,
I have appointments I must keep –
I don't mean to be rude.'

And with these lame excuses
He got onto his feet
And finding servant Dromio
They made a quick retreat.

But more confusion was in store.
They were about to meet
A goldsmith, who came up to them
As they walked down the street.

'I really must be on my way'

'Here's your golden chain,' he said.
'I made it just for you.'
At this Antipholus S replied,
Unsure of what to do,

'There is some error here, I fear,
I'm not the one you seek.'
The goldsmith testily replied,
'You ordered it last week.'

He forced the chain upon the lad
And then he went away.
Antipholus S then said, 'Let's go
And take a ship today.'

He spoke to his man Dromio,
'I do not like it here.
The people all seem crazy –
They're off their heads, I fear.'

Meanwhile, the poor old goldsmith
Was in trouble down the road,
For officers were having words
About some cash he owed.

These chaps were in the process
Of arresting him, but then
Antipholus E came into view –
The goldsmith said, 'Wait, men.

'This man will pay my debt for me,
For I gave him a chain
And if you let me speak to him
I know that he'll explain,

'That it can all be sorted.
He'll pay the cash I owe.'
Antipholus E, when he was asked,
Just didn't want to know.

He said, 'I never had the chain.'
And thus began a row.
The goldsmith remonstrated,
'I gave it you just now.

'You put it in your pocket.'
Antipholus E said, 'No!'
The officers at last declared
That they would have to throw

The goldsmith into jail until
His debts were duly paid.
The goldsmith then with angry words
Endeavoured to persuade

The officers to take in charge
Antipholus E as well.
'He owes me for the chain,' he said,
'So he should share my cell.'

The officers had had enough;
This all must be curtailed,
So they arrested both of them
And took them to be jailed.

But as Antipholus E was dragged
To prison, he then saw
Young Dromio S, his brother's man –
He told him of the score,

And ordered him to go at once
And tell his wife to send
Some money – but poor Dromio S
Just didn't comprehend.

Then thinking that his master
Desired him to return
To Adriana's house, he went –
For he did not discern

This wasn't *his* Antipholus.
So off he duly went,
Although he really didn't know
What all this nonsense meant.

Well, Adriana gave him cash
But as he thus returned
He saw Antipholus (that's S)
Who with confusion burned,

For everywhere he went he found
The folk all called him 'friend';
The kindness people showed to him
He couldn't comprehend.

And so when Dromio S came up
And said, 'My master, pray,
How did you slip the officer?
How did you get away?'

And then went on to add, 'Look here,
I've now got all this dough...'
Antipholus S was forced to think
His servant Dromio

Had really lost the plot for sure,
He stood there quite astounded:
All these crazy goings-on
Had left him quite dumbfounded.

And then to cap the whole thing off
A lady now came up,
Who claimed that this Antipholus
Had been to her to sup.

And then she asked him for a chain
He'd promised as a gift.
He said, 'What are you speaking of?
I just don't get your drift.'

But she continued to insist.
He said she was a fool,
And when she carried on again
He really lost his cool.

He said she was a sorceress.
She countered, 'Where's my ring?'
He answered, 'I have no idea,
For I don't know a thing

'About a ring or who you are.'
And then he ran away.
He wouldn't hear another word
Of what she had to say.

An explanation to all this
Would be in order here –
I must ensure that everything
Makes sense and is quite clear.

When Antipholus E was sent
Packing from his door –
He thought his wife was in a mood,
He was convinced for sure,

It was a silly jealous rant
From his bad-tempered wife.
He thought, 'I'll teach a lesson
She'll remember all her life.'

So he'd gone to the lady
And promised her a chain,
To make his wife behave herself,
Be sensible again.

The chain was one he'd ordered,
Supposed to be a gift
For his own wife, to make amends
For yet another rift.

But in his fit of pique, he'd said
He'd give the chain away
To this good lady, though he guessed
There'd be a price to pay.

He didn't have it on him
But said that he would bring
The chain a little later on –
That's when she gave the ring.

For she was pleased that she would have
A chain – a lovely thing –
And in a passion she had said,
'Here, take my favourite ring.'

So when she had confronted
Antipholus S, she thought
It was his brother, who to her
Seemed sadly fallen short,

For he denied all knowledge
Of the gift he'd promised her –
He really must be mad, she thought
Or just a rotten cur.

At last she had decided
He wasn't only bad...
No, there could be no doubt at all
He'd gone completely mad.

She went to Adriana,
And said, 'It's sad to say,
Your husband has gone crazy –
It happened just today.'

Adriana did not doubt
These words for she knew how
He'd been so strange at dinner
And how with furrowed brow

He'd said he wasn't married,
That she was not his wife,
That he'd not been to Ephesus
Before in all his life.

So, now convinced, she went to him,
Imprisoned in the jail,
And paid the money that was due,
So he was granted bail.

She had her servants tie him up
With ropes, and had him thrown
Into a dim and darkened room,
And left him there alone.

Dromio E was locked up too –
They told the self-same tale –
And though they were locked up at home
It seemed just like the jail.

But then a little later on
Somebody came to tell
That Adriana's husband walked
In town and looked quite well.

And Dromio was with him –
They must have broken loose!
How could this thing have happened?
How did they slip the noose?

When Adriana heard of this
She ran to fetch him home,
Determined she would tie him down
So that he couldn't roam.

She found him by a convent –
That's who she *thought* she saw...
It was, of course, her yet unknown
Bewildered brother-in-law.

She had her servants tie him up

Antipholus S was standing there
With Dromio S as well.
The goldsmith – he was giving
Antipholus sheer hell.

They'd let the goldsmith out of jail,
And now he cried, 'By heck,
Why did you so deny you had
That chain that's round your neck?'

Antipholus S was saying,
'You freely gave this chain,
And since that hour I've never clapped
My eyes on you again.'

Adriana then appeared
Right before their eyes,
And she had brought along with her
A bunch of burly guys.

They tried to grab Antipholus,
His servant Dromio too.
They ran into the convent,
The smartest thing to do.

They begged for shelter in the shrine;
The abbess then came out
To ascertain what all the fuss
Outside had been about.

She was a wise old lady –
Said she was not prepared
To give the two men up just yet,
Who both seemed very scared,

Until she'd heard the details
Of what they were accused.
Adriana was annoyed –
No, she was not amused.

She said her faithless husband
Had completely lost his mind.
'It really is his fault that he
Is in this awful bind.'

The abbess sighed, 'You should have nagged
If he has been untrue.
You should have told him all the time
It's not the thing to do.'

'I did! I did!' the wife replied.
'I told him all the time.
I said that doing what he did
Was tantamount to crime.

'I told him off when in our bed,
And when he tried to eat.
I told him off throughout the meal,
Until he left his seat.

'And when alone, I told him,'
This Adriana said,
'What a rotten man he was,
The worthless life he led.

'And when we were in company
I still would have a go –
Oh yes, sweet abbess, in all truth
I really let him know.'

The abbess had found out for sure
What drove the poor man mad.
She said, 'I think you've acted
In a way that's very bad.

'These actions you've recounted,
Done time and time again,
Would drive a really noble man
Around the bend – insane!

'A jealous woman is, for sure,
Much worse, I say, forsooth,
Than deadly poison deep within
A mad dog's fearsome tooth.'

Her sister, Luciana, said,
'Why take this lying down?'
But Adriana thus replied
With an embarrassed frown,

'The abbess speaks the truth – I see
The error of my ways,
For I have acted woefully
On very many days.'

But still she said, 'My husband,
Who's cowering in there
Should now be handed over
Into my loving care.'

The abbess wouldn't give him up;
She really was a gem.
She said, 'I will take care of him.'
Then closed her gates on them.

As all this had been happening,
We sadly have to say,
Egeon's single day of grace
Had quickly slipped away.

And he would die at sunset,
They'd execute him there.
Close to the convent he'd be told
To make his final prayer.

But at that very moment
Some people came along:
It was the Duke and Egeon,
Accompanied by a throng.

When Adriana saw the Duke
She stopped him in his track.
'The abbess has my husband
And she will not give him back.'

But as she spoke, who should appear,
Quite sane and looking spruce –
Her husband and his Dromio,
The pair had just got loose.

He complained, as well he might,
He told the Duke his tale,
How his bad wife had called him mad...
Oh, how he did regale

The Duke with all the awful things
He said that he'd been through,
How he'd been locked up on his own –
Of how he broke out too.

As he spoke out, his wife stood by,
Surprise upon her face.
Was this her husband standing here
Or just one more nutcase?

For she believed her husband
Was in the convent there;
She shook her head and wrung her hands
In her perplexed despair.

Egeon looked upon his son
And thought he was no other
Than that same boy who'd left his home
To find his mum and brother.

But this of course, was not the case;
It was Antipholus E
To whom he spoke and who replied,
'You are not known to me.'

Egeon was astonished
To be denied this way,
When he said, 'We have not met.'
What could Egeon say?

He thought his son was just borne down
By some strange silly whim,
That some weird illness was the cause
Of his not knowing him.

But as he spoke, the convent door
Was opened – there appeared
The abbess with the two young men;
Now this was really weird.

Everyone there present, gasped.
Could all of this be true?
And Adriana saw she had
Not one spouse there, but two!

There stood Antipholus himself
And Dromio S as well.
The Duke recalled Egeon's tale –
When he had heard him tell

The details of the shipwreck –
So said, 'It seems to me
The sons of this poor man right here
Are who these boys must be.'

Oh what a joyful moment
As Egeon hugged his sons,
A reunion quite as memorable
As history's greatest ones.

But then the lady abbess
Completed all their joys.
She said, 'I am Egeon's wife
And these are my two boys,'

Explaining that the fishermen,
Who'd rescued them, all three,
Had sold the boys when they arrived
Safely in port from sea.

And so she'd joined the convent
To ease her desperate grief,
And here she'd found some solace
And sanctified relief.

In time by holy conduct,
Avoiding selfish ploys,
She'd been elected abbess,
And thus had found her boys.

Amid these joyful happenings
One thing they all forgot
Was that poor, old Egeon
Was still in quite a spot:

He was still under sentence,
And could quite soon be dead.
Antipholus E spoke out at once:
'I'll pay the fee,' he said.

The Duke though would have none of it.
'He's pardoned,' then he cried.
'He is excused the thousand marks –
Proclaim it far and wide.

'And he shall be a free man
Within our country here,
And from this moment on he is
Completely in the clear.'

They walked into the convent,
A most contented band.
Everyone was happy that
The fates had played this hand,

And brought them all together,
A family again,
And so this doesn't leave too much
For us now to explain.

The Dromios, of course, were pleased,
Each one to meet his twin;
The pair of them just walked around
With a perpetual grin.

And both said that they'd never seen,
In life or picture books,
A person like their brother there
Who had such handsome looks.

And Adriana, for her part,
Showed jealousy no more;
She listened to the council of
Her gracious mother-in-law.

Antipholus S, as we all know
Had had a roving eye;
Since seeing Luciana
He'd been a love-sick guy.

So he proposed she marry him.
And, guess what! She said, 'Yes!'
And thus their marriage marked the end
Of all this silly mess.

Egeon lived on happily
For many fruitful years,
Surrounded by his family,
With no more grief or tears.

No more wandering the world
With all its many terrors,
And no more time confused within
A comedy of errors.

'*I challenge you, good sir*'

RICHARD THE SECOND

Kings have many duties
That need attending to,
And dealing with high treason
Is one thing they *must* do.

And thus it was on one such day,
Richard the Second found
He had to act as arbiter,
He had there to expound

And give a strong, sound judgement
And try to wisely gauge
The truth about a great dispute
That at the time did rage.

Henry Bolingbroke, the son
Of Lancaster's bold Duke,
Arraigned another to the King
And would not brook rebuke.

This was the Duke of Norfolk,
Thomas Mowbray, who now stood
Before the court and was accused
Of treason and falsehood.

Bolingbroke now made the case,
Mowbray he called a cur,
And threw his glove upon the floor:
'I challenge you, good sir.

'For you have been dishonest,
Misused our dear King's cash.'
Oh, how he ranted and then raved,
Oh, how his eyes did flash.

And then his anger boiled anew –
He called him an impostor,
And said, 'You are the one who's killed
Our much loved Duke of Gloucester.'

Mowbray denied this vehemently,
He said it was a lie.
He threw his glove down too and said,
'For that I'll see you die.'

King Richard hated this discord,
He liked things to be nice.
He pleaded with young Henry's dad
To give his son advice.

'My gracious Duke of Lancaster,
Please beg your son be calm,
Tell him to take his challenge back,
For he may do much harm.

'And Mowbray, think again, good sir,
Of what you plan to do;
Fighting with bold Bolingbroke
Could mean swift death for you.'

Mowbray says that he's determined
To duel for his good name,
And Bolingbroke declares that he
Intends to do the same.

He said, 'If I do less than this
'Twould wound my honour, Sire.'
King Richard sees there is no way
That he can quench this fire.

And so with resignation
He declares that they must fight:
'Let chivalry determine now
Which one of you is right.'

Now this may seem straightforward,
But all's not as it seems,
For people think that Richard was
Involved in Mowbray's schemes.

They think that Richard secretly
Connived in Gloucester's end;
They think that Mowbray is the King's
Close confidant and friend.

So Richard, though he is prepared
Thus to support the duel,
Is really part of all this mess,
For he has helped to fuel

The argument now raging,
And so he feels concerned
The blood that's on his royal hands
Might somehow be discerned.

Later, the Duke of Lancaster,
Called John of Gaunt, by some,
Is having a hard time of it –
He's looking very glum:

The Duchess of dead Gloucester
Is in an awful rage;
There are no words that he can find
To calm her or assuage

The awful grief and wrath she feels.
She says, 'You are his brother.
You should demand revenge for this,
Far more than any other.'

But John of Gaunt averts his eyes
And solemnly looks down,
For he believes in monarchy –
He won't usurp the crown.

He'll not avenge his brother's death,
He will not ride roughshod,
Against the King, for he believes
He's been put there by God.

The Duchess feels let down by this
And vows, with tearful eye,
'In desolation I now leave,
For home – and there I'll die.'

The story moves to Coventry
And in the morning mists
We spot the great arena
Wherein we see the lists.

And here the trial by combat
Is scheduled to take place,
With deadly weapons of the time:
The sword, the axe, the mace.

And then the mists evaporate,
The morning dew dries out,
And from the corner of the field
Comes an almighty shout.

'Long live the King! Here comes the King!'
And into that vast field
King Richard rides with sword in hand
Along with his great shield.

He takes his place upon a throne
And then, with loyal zeal,
Mowbray and Bolingbroke approach –
Before the King they kneel.

They each declare their loyalty
To this their royal Lord,
Heads bowed in supplication,
Each hand upon his sword.

And then the accusation
Is read for all to hear;
Then Mowbray's strong denial
Of this ignoble smear.

So now these enemies prepare
To test their strength and might.
But suddenly King Richard says,
'I'll not allow this fight.

'I've changed my mind – it is my will,
It is my kingly right.
I've now decided both of you
Are banished from my sight.

'Mowbray, you will leave our realm
And nevermore return;
You'll never see this land again,
However much you yearn.

'And, Bolingbroke, I banish you,
Though truthfully with tears,
Begone from this fair land at once
For all of six long years.'

Old John of Gaunt was mortified
To hear his poor son's fate,
But hid his grief for he remained
True to the King and state.

And later on he says goodbye
To his departing lad,
And urges him to realise
That things are not too bad.

'For everywhere that Heaven's eye
Does visit in a day
Are happy havens for wise men,
And this I also say:

'Waste not your time in thinking
Of where you may have been,
But look ahead to where you go,
That future yet unseen.'

But Bolingbroke was not impressed
With all this clever stuff.
He left his dad and hurried off
In something of a huff.

Meanwhile, King Richard meets his court.
He says, 'Bold Henry shone
Within the heart of common folk –
I'm so relieved he's gone.'

But then he moved on swiftly,
For he had just had word
Of yet more strife and trouble
That had right then occurred.

He said, 'To this rebellion,
In Ireland we must go.'
A courtier ventured, 'But my Lord
Our funds have run too low.

'It costs a lot of money
To run a decent court –
We'll have to raise the taxes.
I'll draw up a report

'To show how it can be achieved,
And how Your Grace can get
An army to put down this foe –
We'll beat these rebels yet.'

But then news came that John of Gaunt
Was ill and nearing death.
Richard declared, 'Let's go – and hope
We miss his final breath.'

How very mean and callous!
But Richard now can see,
With poor old John's approaching death,
A way to raise the fee

That he must pay to form a force
To quell the Irish mob.
He rubs his hands and smiles and says,
'Well this is just the job.

'We'll grab his lands and property
Once good old John is dead,
But for the moment let us go
To visit his death bed.'

Old John of Gaunt is fading fast;
He sits there in a swoon.
Then he comes round and says to York,
'I hope the King comes soon.

'For I would have some words with him
And make him change his mind,
Show him the way to govern well
And leave his past behind.

'And I will tell the King the truth
And make my feelings plain,
For they speak truly who thus breathe
Their dying words in pain.'

The Duke of York sighed deeply.
'He'll not admit his crime,
Or any of his failings –
You'll only waste your time.'

But John of Gaunt will not be swayed
For he loves England so,
And says, 'I must speak out, dear York –
And shall before I go.

'For our beloved England,
Surrounded by the sea,
Has always seemed like Eden –
A paradise to me.

'For she is like a fortress
Within this silver sea,
Protected on all sides and safe
For all eternity

'Against all foul infections
And cruel hand of war,
Envied by less happy lands
That lie beyond our shore.

'This earth, this realm, this England,
This womb of royal kings,
Famed by their birth and much renowned
For such courageous things.

'Acclaimed for deeds of chivalry
And Christian service too,
This land that's known throughout the world
For all that's good and true.

'This blessed home of such dear souls,
This dear beloved land
Is now leased out to one who has
A most unworthy hand.

'I love this blessed plot of ours,
This noble England here,
This dearest land, this sceptred Isle,
And that is why I fear

'For what will happen when I die…
If only England, brave,
Would vanquish scandal, once these bones
Are laid within their grave.

'For then I'd die a happy man
And with my final breath,
Would welcome gratefully the hand
Of cold, ensuing death.'

Just as he finished this lament
King Richard walked right in.
Gaunt greeted him with scant respect
And gave a watery grin.

He then within a moment
Began a bold attack:
'You gild yourself with flatterers –
A vain, unwholesome pack.'

And then he let him have it,
For as his death was near
I guess it's fair to say he felt
He had no more to fear.

He told the King he was no good,
He really put him down.
He said, 'You are not fit to wear
Beloved England's crown.'

He told the King he was no good

Richard wasn't taking this;
Old Gaunt had gone too far.
He said, 'I'd have your head chopped off
If you weren't who you are.'

But John of Gaunt would not be cowed.
He said, 'Your bile did foster
Ambition, which then made you kill
My brother, Duke of Gloucester.

'So let these words live after me
And your tormentors be;
Let them ferment within your mind,
As constant company.'

197

And then his head dropped forward
And with a feeble wave,
He said, 'Convey me to my bed,
Then hence unto my grave.'

Now shortly after this debate,
This monumental row,
The Duke, despairing, passed away –
And Richard kept his vow

To grab all Gaunt's possessions.
He just ignored the law;
He wanted all the wealth and lands
To help finance his war.

The Duke of York spoke out and said,
'This action is not fair,
For Bolingbroke owns all of this –
He is the rightful heir.

'And by your actions you will bring
Great danger on your head,
For this will mean you'll never more
Sleep easy in your bed.

'And I shall also prophesy
That great disorder starts
From this time onwards, for you'll lose
All true and loyal hearts.'

Richard went to Ireland
To sort the rebels out.
He was confident he'd win,
Sure it would be a rout.

But Henry Bolingbroke has heard
Of how the King has taken
His lands and his inheritance –
He's very badly shaken.

Angry too, it's fair to say,
For this is quite outrageous.
But Henry is a bold, brave man;
He really is courageous.

And so he sails for England now
And brings an army too.
He's quite determined in his mind
On what he means to do.

He'll take the crown, for now he feels
For Richard mere contempt;
He'll end up King of England yet,
Or die in the attempt.

Richard returns from Ireland –
But he's delayed too long,
And by the time he gets back home
Affairs are going wrong.

Supporters have grown tired
Of all this hanging round.
Within his realm uneasiness
And discontent abound.

He is weak and doesn't like
The way things are unfolding;
He's really most unhappy at
The cards he finds he's holding.

Henry's forces gather pace,
They're gaining much support,
And as they win the people's heart
Poor Richard grows distraught.

His forces are in disarray;
It seems that victory
Will go to Henry Bolingbroke
Who promises to be

A good and noble King to all.
King Richard's time is past;
It's time for England to be led
By someone strong at last.

It all comes to a head one day:
The King is safe inside
Flint Castle, where he's made the choice
His court will now reside.

Richard says, 'I do believe
The waters of the sea
Do not have the power to wash
The holy balm from me,

'The sacred oil that marked me King,
That crowned me long ago.
I do not have to waste my time
In fearing any foe.'

But when Earl Salisbury came in,
His hubris was converted
To swift despair when he was told
The Welsh had just deserted.

'Is now my kingdom lost?' he cried.
'Is this the end of me?
I am in truth then but a man,
Despite my majesty.

'For now it seems that we will pass
At once, with no delay,
From Richard's dark depressing night
To Bolingbroke's fair day.'

Henry's forces now approach –
Surround the castle walls.
And there it is the strangest thing
Quite suddenly befalls.

For first of all brave Bolingbroke
Says all he wants is this:
To have his lands and wealth returned,
Then he'll be pleased to kiss

The royal hand of Richard there,
Call him his noble Lord...
The King says he'll agree, of course,
To end all this discord.

But once this is agreed it seems
The King's will just breaks down,
He says he'll abdicate the throne,
Relinquish England's crown.

And asks, 'Will gracious Henry
Agree, and tell no lies,
To let me go on living
Until poor Richard dies?

'For then I'll give my crown to him,'
He said with furrowed brow.
'I will submit, I'll give my throne -
And I will do it now.

'I'll exchange my jewels for beads,
My palace I will give
For a humble hermitage,
And there I'll gladly live.

'My sceptre here shall be replaced,'
He said with tired laugh.
'By something more befitting like
A palmer's walking staff.

'And when I die, I humbly say
I really do not crave
A monument, just place me in
A modest, little grave.'

So we can see that Richard thought
That he could never win,
And so he made his mind up then
To abdicate – give in!

A meeting then is organised
And, o'er a glass of wine,
King Richard in dejection says
That he will now resign.

In one dramatic gesture
He makes this sad request:
'Bring me a mirror here at once.'
They think it is a jest.

But when the mirror's brought he looks,
And says with tired groan,
'Is this the face that gazed upon
All others from the throne?

'It's hard now to believe it so,
For who would ever think
That, like the sun, this face did make
All rapt beholders blink.'

And then he dashed the mirror,
With anger, to the floor.
'See how great sorrow wrecks a face;
I'll not look anymore.'

They asked him where he wished to go,
Where would he rest his head.
'In any place beyond your sight,'
Defiantly he said.

This angered Henry very much
And so, within the hour,
The erstwhile King was led away
And thrown into the Tower,

Where, some time later, he was told,
'You're going to be sent
To Pomfret Castle, in the north...'
And that is where he went.

Richard was a sorry sight.
Is this what he deserved?
He may have been a weak, vain King,
For so we have observed.

But in reality his sin
Was just to be a clown.
Should silliness and vanity
Cause him to lose his crown?

But there is worse to follow.
Things will be getting rough
For Richard, as King Henry
Has nearly had enough.

And one day in his court he cries,
So everyone can hear,
'Have I no friend who'll rid me of
This dreadful, living fear?'

Sir Piers of Exton who was there
Is sure that this remark
Is Henry's plea for some good friend
To steal, when it is dark,

To Pomfret castle and there bring
A swift and certain end
To Richard – he believes that thus
He'll make the King his friend.

In Pomfret Castle, Richard,
A prisoner, now we see.
He says, 'I wasted time before
But now time wasteth me.

'My hours all are faded
And withered to this sum.
I had my day but now I see
That Bolingbroke's has come.'

And as he uttered these sad words
The prison door was flung
Wide open – 'What is this?' he cried...
A voice called, 'Hold your tongue!'

Sir Piers of Exton then came in
With others at his side,
And Richard saw at once that they
Intended regicide.

He snatched the sword from one of them
And with a mighty thrust,
Sent the assailant to his death –
The fellow bit the dust.

King Richard cried, 'Foul villain,
As you draw your final breath,
Know your own hand has thus supplied
Your instrument of death.'

And then he killed a second man,
And as the poor man fell
King Richard breathed, 'Go now and fill
Another room in hell.'

He fought them bravely but, alas,
It was to no avail;
There was no place to run and hide
In Pomfret Castle jail.

They hacked at poor King Richard
And with his dying breath
He prophesied the injury
To England by his death.

He cried aloud in agony,
'Exton, your foul hand
Has with the spilling of my blood
Stained all King Henry's land.

'And so I say, rise up my soul
To Heaven, way on high,
While my gross flesh sink downward now
Upon the earth to die.'

And then within a pool of gore
Poor, wronged King Richard died,
A victim of his majesty
And of his kingly pride.

They took King Richard's body then,
A King without a crown,
To Henry at the castle keep
In royal Windsor town.

They hacked at poor King Richard

Exton told King Henry there,
'Upon this funeral bier,
I bring the lifeless body
Of your now buried fear.

'Here lies your greatest enemy,
Here lies the end you sought.
The scoundrel Richard's body thus
Have I now hither brought.'

When Henry saw cold Richard there
His feelings were all mixed,
In some respects he was quite glad
The problem had been fixed.

But he told Exton angrily,
'I can't condone this plot.
It isn't what this King desired
And so I thank thee not.

'For by this deed of villainy
With your foul, wicked hand,
You've wrought a deed of slander on
My head and on this land.'

Exton cried, 'I did this deed –
Wielded my loyal sword,
Because I heard from your own mouth
You wished him dead, my Lord.'

Henry replied, 'It was not so –
Not what I meant,' he said.
'I didn't want him murdered, though
It's true, I craved him dead.

'For though I hate the murderer,
I love him murdered, so
I really can't complain too much.'
And he let Exton go.

And then he banished shamed Sir Piers,
He also made it clear,
That he himself was free of blame,
But – to allay his fear

That he would one day rot in hell –
He vowed that he would go
Crusading to the Holy Land;
Then everyone would know

He'd wiped the slate entirely clean
For this horrendous thing.
He'd make amends for murdering
A true, anointed King.

The youths are stuck in jail

THE TWO NOBLE KINSMEN

The Duke of Athens, Theseus,
Got in a fight one day.
It happened as he journeyed home
After some time away.

He fought the court of ancient Thebes,
It was a raging sight –
But after many twists and turns
Brave Theseus won the fight.

He took some captives home with him,
He took them as his prize,
And in amongst them were a pair
Of cousins – two young guys.

Their uncle was King Creon;
In Thebes he was the boss.
These Princes were a mite upset,
Fed up and very cross

At being taken prisoner.
They cursed and swore out loud
For, being royal Princes,
They both were very proud.

So this is where our tale begins:
The youths are stuck in jail.
The prison's grim, the walls are thick,
The air is very stale.

But Palamon at length declares,
'Arcite, my dear friend,
I do not think that anything
Could make our friendship end.

'For we are really quite as close
As two good friends could be.'
Arcite smiled, 'My cousin, dear,
I readily agree.'

Then Palamon, on looking down
Between the prison bars,
Beheld a sight more beautiful
Than heaven's brightest stars.

For in a garden, far below,
There walked Emilia fair,
And when he saw her, Palamon
Could only stop and stare.

She won his heart immediately
He saw her from above.
He knew she was the one for him –
The Prince was deep in love.

Emilia was the sister to
The Duke of Athens' bride;
She'd come to join her sister,
To be right by her side.

As Palamon stood there transfixed,
Amazement on his face,
Arcite said, 'Let's have a look.
Move over – make some space.'

He too looked down from way above
And when he saw the girl
Her beauty also won his heart,
His feelings were a-whirl.

She was the prettiest creature
His eyes had ever seen,
For she was gentle, fair of face,
Most gracious and serene.

She looked so small and dainty as
She walked there on her own;
Arcite, in that moment vowed,
'She will be mine alone.'

But Palamon was quick to say –
His heart was fit to burst –
'She's mine for it was I who saw
This lovely lady first.'

'That doesn't mean a thing at all,'
Arcite then cried out.
Palamon then yelled as well –
They both began to shout.

And in a moment all was changed:
From being friends they were
Reduced to calling names – such as
'You dog!', 'You fiend!', 'You cur!'

They argued then most angrily
Within their little cell.
These erstwhile friends gave each to each
All kinds of verbal hell.

But then the jailor came to say
The Duke desired to speak
To young Arcite, who, of course
Thought, 'Now I'm up the creek.'

He felt it meant more trouble,
So he was filled with fear,
And he did not expect to learn
What he was set to hear.

The Duke said, 'You can go at once.
Get out of Athens now.
But if we find you here again,
This thing I firmly vow:

'That it will be the worst for you.
Now, my young Prince, depart!'
So poor Arcite turned to leave
With very heavy heart.

For he now left Emilia –
He didn't want to go.
He envied Palamon so much
He saw him as his foe,

For Palamon could see the girl,
The object of their love,
By gazing from the window there,
Which looked down from above.

Arcite vowed right there and then,
'I'd much prefer to be
In Palamon's grim prison cell
Than be outside and free.'

So, feeling in this way, I guess
It comes as no surprise,
Arcite thought that he'd return,
But dressed in a disguise.

He met some folk along the road,
All going to a fair –
One organised by Theseus.
He thought, 'I'll join them there.'

So, in disguise, he made his way
Straight back to Athens, then
He joined in all the sporting trials
Against the strongest men.

He entered each event and thus
He took on everyone,
And he came out on top each time...
Yes, every time he won.

Theseus was so impressed.
He thought, 'This lad's a star.
He's really quite exceptional,
The very best by far.

'So he deserves a special place
Within my service here.'
He gave Arcite then a post
That made the young Prince cheer.

He was appointed servant to
His own true heart's desire:
Emilia – his one true love,
Who'd set his heart on fire.

But what of poor young Palamon
Within that jail so grim?
How has *he* been getting on?
What's happening to him?

Well, he has had a bit of luck:
The jailor's daughter there
Has told him that she loves him so
And that it isn't fair

That he's imprisoned and she says,
'My darling, do not fear.
I'll find you food and clothing,
Then get you out of here.'

And she was faithful to her word –
She got the poor chap out
By taking full advantage
Of a jailor's daughter's clout.

The fair was still progressing...
Arcite felt such joy
To be there with Emilia
And serve in her employ.

But then one day he felt a shove,
Someone gave him a push,
And turning he saw Palamon
Emerging from a bush.

He still was locked in shackles –
A prisoner on the run –
While his cousin, Arcite,
Was there just having fun.

It only took a moment
Before they both grew rude
And, shouting at each other then,
Renewed their angry feud.

They shouted at each other
Till they were out of breath,
And then agreed that they would fight
Each other to the death.

It seemed to them the only way
To settle their dispute,
For it would leave one man alone
To prosecute his suit.

Arcite said, 'Before we fight
You must consume some food,
And we must get those shackles off –
They'll hinder and protrude.

'For if we are to fight we must
Ensure the fight is fair.'
Although their course was set they were
A very courteous pair.

For when they donned their armour
Each one was pleasant to
The other as each kindly asked,
'Can I give help to you?

'And please say if your mail's too tight.
And are your gloves OK?
And if your armour's chafing you
Don't hesitate to say.'

Then finally they both were set,
Each ready for a fight.
But then, as if from nowhere,
The Duke came into sight.

He and his court were hunting.
'What's going on?' he cried.
The two young Princes both spoke out.
You'd think they would have lied,

But they told Theseus the truth;
They told him who they were.
'We're fighting for Emilia,
We're both in love with her.'

The Duke was very angry,
His face turned brightest red.
'I sentence both of you to die,'
He very coldly said.

Emilia, who was standing there,
Gasped in distress and sighed.
'Oh please don't kill them. Banish them...
Oh please, my Lord,' she cried.

But Theseus then turned and said
Some words he thought were wise:
A smart solution, so he thought,
Which gave her a surprise.

'I'll tell you what we'll do,' he said.
'They're young and should have wives,
And you are also young and wish
To save these Princes' lives.

'So I propose that you should take
One of these fellows here
To be your partner.' She replied,
'I cannot choose, I fear.

'For they are both so excellent,
It would be hard to voice
A preference – I really can't
Begin to make a choice.'

So Theseus spoke out again:
'We'll settle this my way.
You'll both return to Athens in
Just one month from today.

'And you will fight a duel here.
The winner,' he then said,
'Will marry fair Emilia –
The other lose his head!'

A month passed by and all alone,
Within her palace room,
Emilia gazed at pictures
Of the Princes, both of whom

She held in high affection.
They each displayed such grace;
And both of them were manly
And, oh, so fine of face.

But now the Princes have returned,
Emilia kneels and prays.
'Please let the winner be the one
Who loves me best,' she says.

She cannot stand to watch the fight,
But still retains her poise
As to her anxious ears is brought
The din and clashing noise,

As mighty sword strikes mighty sword,
As mace pounds on a shield –
And from the tumult it is clear
That neither Prince will yield.

But then she hears a lusty shout.
So who has won the fight?
She thinks that Palamon has won,
But finds she isn't right.

Arcite comes before her
And bows down very low.
He says, 'Sweet lady, I now claim
The right to be your beau.'

But as he celebrates the fact
That he has won her love,
Poor Palamon is on his knees
In prayer to heaven above.

For he is now about to die,
He is about to feel
The axe-man's blade across his neck...
This was, we know, the deal.

And though Emilia pleaded long
With every single breath,
The Duke of Athens said that nought
Could save him now from death.

And so the valiant Palamon,
Bravely, but in shock,
Is led to execution
To face the axe-man's block.

He holds himself erect and tall,
Determined that he'll die
Like one who's born of royal blood.
He looks up to the sky

And says a heartfelt prayer, and then,
With but a little sigh,
He says, 'My dear Emilia,
I bid you now goodbye.'

But at the very moment
That he prepares to die,
When he has made his final prayer,
He hears a garbled cry.

A messenger has come with news.
The man cries in remorse:
'Arcite has been injured,
He's fallen from his horse.'

And so brave Palamon is spared.
He goes to his old friend,
And there it is he witnesses
Arcite's dismal end.

And so brave Palamon is spared

Before he dies Arcite says,
'Now I forsake this life,
You must take fair Emilia
For your beloved wife.

'I ask of you but one small thing
So I can die in bliss:
Emilia, please, I beg you now,
Give me one final kiss.'

And thus the poor Arcite died.
And everyone agreed
It was a tragedy the Prince
Had fallen from his steed.

But now that he was dead it seemed
To make but common sense
Emilia should have Palamon
By way of recompense.

The Duke agreed their marriage;
And then he did proclaim,
That this time, fickle fortune
Had played a subtle game.

'For it is very strange indeed
That things should end this way,
But one fact yet remains the same –
We'll have a wedding day!'

He was a very haughty man

228

CORIOLANUS

So here's the situation,
We're once again in Rome,
And there is trouble brewing
As we begin this tome.

The city's short of food,
The masses are fed up:
No bread to put upon a plate,
No cider for a cup.

And as their stomachs rumble
So does their rage and ire;
They're getting really angry,
Emotions are on fire.

And thus it doesn't take too long
For this their scanty diet
To be the cause of all of Rome
Erupting in a riot.

And like all angry masses
They need to have a name
At which they can direct their rage,
On which to lay the blame.

And so these Roman citizens,
Who have enormous chips
Upon their shoulders, all unite –
One name is on their lips.

They cry out, 'Caius Martius!
Everything's his fault.'
But Menenius speaks to them,
He tells them all to halt.

He says that no-one is to blame,
He says, 'It is the gods
Who've brought this famine onto Rome.'
He sees a few slight nods

And thinks he might be turning
The Roman crowd around;
Perhaps with some more argument
He'll gain a mite more ground.

'If you believe the senate
Has a belly, fat and gross,
Just remember this one fact
Before being bellicose:

'That belly nurtures everyone –
Surely this you know –
Through levels of society,
Right to the people's toe.'

Then Caius Martius arrives,
Upon his face a sneer;
He was a very haughty man –
Quite up himself, I fear.

His manner is unhelpful,
It does no good at all,
Belligerent and quite stuck up,
And then he has the gall

To say that all the rioters
Should there and then be strung
Right up onto the highest tree,
And very quickly hung.

This didn't go down well at all –
He wasn't finished yet...
He then began to criticize
Two men he'd hardly met:

Sicinius and Brutus – these
Had been the people's choice
To serve them in the Senate,
And there to be their voice.

But Martius just mocked them
And said they were no good –
Not a clever thing to do
In view of how things stood.

But then some fearful news arrived,
Another bitter blow,
The Volsces had now taken arms –
They are Rome's greatest foe.

And once again they're keen to fight,
Emotions all a-foam;
They are intent and quite resolved
To challenge mighty Rome.

There is only one man there
To lead the Roman cause,
And so the people's anger
Now turns to loud applause.

For Martius is the man to lead –
He's saved Rome in the past.
His bravery is legendary,
His experience is vast.

So Martius prepares to fight.
His wife – Virgilia, fair –
Is frightened for his safety
And frets and worries there.

Volumnia, his mother,
Merely scoffs and says she's crass:
'You are a spineless, stupid thing,
A really silly lass.

'For Martius was raised to be
A soldier with no fear,
So don't go carrying on this way,
It's unbecoming, dear.

'The many wounds he's suffered
Show his great strength and might,
He's a warrior through and through,
My son was born to fight!'

So we go to Corioli,
And it's there we'll find
Aufidius, the Volscian,
And he is of a mind

To thrash proud Caius Martius –
For he's always lost before –
Aufidius was determined
He'd win this brand new war.

And so they met in battle –
It was a grisly fight.
The Volscians came out rather well
Against the Roman might.

The Romans grew quite tired,
Almost gave up the ghost.
Martius had to remonstrate
To keep them at their post.

But through the heat of battle
Came Martius like a flood;
He wields his sword – he's covered
From head to toe in blood.

He is a raging, forceful sight,
His courage just won't crack,
And as the Romans thought they'd lost,
He shouted out, 'Attack!'

All in the heat of battle
He then came face to face
With bold Aufidius – whom he fought,
With sword and whirling mace.

Martius would have beaten him –
He was the better sword –
But Volscian soldiers intervened
And bravely saved their Lord.

The battle now had turned around,
The Volscians on the run,
So once again the Romans
And Martius had won.

He then came face to face
With bold Aufidius – whom he fought

The generals, Cominius
And Lartius, both said,
They'd only won because they'd had
Brave Martius at their head.

'And so in recognition
Of our victory today,
Martius shall evermore
Be known a different way.

'We've fought at Corioli
And won this victory,
And so forever from this day
Coriolanus he shall be.'

And then they made their way to Rome.
Aufidius, for his part,
Fled the field and vowed that he
Would make another start,

So he could be avenged some day
On this his fearsome foe,
He was determined and resolved
He'd have another go!

When Coriolanus got back home
His mother was so proud –
She wasn't one to wear success
Beneath a modest shroud.

She boasted, telling everyone:
'My boy's the best of stars
For he has added two more wounds
To all his other scars.'

She wasn't like most mothers –
The more scrapes he got in,
The more she was elated,
The bigger was her grin.

But then the word was spread around,
That he would now become
A Consul – for his victory.
This really pleased his mum.

Such a tremendous honour,
But very much deserved;
Coriolanus always did
His duty – never swerved.

But when the news was broken
Some thought the deed amiss.
Sicinius said to Brutus,
'We must prevent all this.'

Before Coriolanus
Could claim a Consul's crown
There was a deed that he must do
Which really made him frown.

Before the people he must go,
So all of them could see,
Dressed in the customary robe:
'Gown of humility'.

It was the Roman custom,
And nothing else would do:
Before he was made Consul
He'd have to see it through.

He despised the very thought
Of wearing this great cloak,
But it was what new Consuls did,
When they went out and spoke.

He went into the Forum
And told the gathered faction,
'I should be judged by what I've done;
I am a man of action.'

He then said just about enough,
And not one sentence more,
As was required by decency
And by the Senate's law.

238

He had no time for common folk,
He held them in disdain;
As he withdrew he quietly said,
'I won't do that again.'

He couldn't wait to leave the square
And to remove the cloak,
Frustrated now with everything,
A most unhappy bloke.

Once he had left, his enemies
Began to make a fuss;
Brutus and Sicinius said,
'He's got no time for us.'

They urged the people to withdraw
The recent great promotion
Of Consul Coriolanus
And stirred up a commotion.

Coriolanus now is told
Aufidius has retreated
To Antium, and won't accept
That he has been defeated.

He's gathering more soldiers
And trouble is in store –
Aufidius is preparing
For yet another war.

Meanwhile Coriolanus
Is met and roughly greeted
By Brutus and Sicinius
And words get quickly heated.

The two aggressive commoners
Remind the general that
He's a servant of the people
And not some grand 'fat cat'.

Coriolanus looks on them
With his superior air,
Regarding them disdainfully,
While they just stand and stare.

The general in his haughty way
Says, 'You're a sorry shower.
I couldn't give a fig about
This talk of people power.'

Their eyes ignite with hatred,
And Brutus, there and then,
Said, 'Don't you speak to us like that.'
And summoned up some men.

They tried then to arrest him
But Coriolanus, he
Just drew his sword and proudly said,
'You do not frighten me.'

The citizens quite soon dispersed,
All of their own accord;
They didn't like the look at all
Of his enormous sword.

Coriolanus made his way
Back to his home again.
His pushy mother waiting there,
Said, 'You are much too vain.

'If you would be a Consul
You've got to learn to feign
Humility and humble ways –
I know it is a pain,

'But this will be the only way
To gain your heart's desire;
You won't get anywhere at all
By raising people's ire.

'You've got a lot to learn, my son,'
She said with serious sigh.
'If you expect to gain your goal
You've got to learn to lie.'

Finally the penny dropped
Into the general's head.
'I'll feign a harlot's spirit
And flatter them,' he said.

Returning to the Forum,
He'd now made up his mind
To give the people what they want;
He left his pride behind.

But before he had the chance
To flatter or beguile
He found that his two enemies
Had been there for a while.

Sicinius and Brutus
Had stirred the crowd and so
The multitude all gathered there
Just didn't want to know.

And though bold Coriolanus
Did everything to cater
To citizens in fickle mood,
They all yelled at him: 'Traitor!'

Sicinius then shouted,
'You're a tyrant and that's why
We know that you'd betray us
And why we know you lie.'

Coriolanus was outraged
To be addressed this way;
The crowd there wouldn't listen,
For all they did was bay.

And then proud Coriolanus
Replied, 'You're such small fry,
Your approbation I'll not seek,
In fact I'd rather die.'

The crowd all rose together.
'Kill him,' some of them cried.
Coriolanus looked at them
With scorn, contempt and pride.

The tribunes then came forward.
'You're banished,' they both said.
'Get out of Rome this instant,
Or you will end up dead.'

Coriolanus, with some cause,
Cursed them and yelled and raved
Against the citizens of Rome
Whom he'd so often saved.

He thought them all ungrateful –
The greatest of all sins –
To think how many times he'd saved
Their cowardly rotten skins!

And so proud Coriolanus
Tried bravely to dispel
All worries for his future
As he made his grand farewell.

His family and some firm friends,
All in a sorry state,
Have come to bid a fond goodbye
At Rome's great eastern gate.

But after he has left them all
His mother has a go
At Brutus and Sicinius –
She really let them know,

Exactly what she thought of them;
You should have heard her tell
The motley pair just what she thought –
You should have heard her yell.

They didn't give a fig for her
And said that on the whole,
Now things would be much better
With the people in control.

Meanwhile Coriolanus
Did something that he loathed:
He dressed in shabby garments –
As a beggar, he was clothed.

Then to Aufidius's house
He boldly bent his tread –
Yes, to his old arch-enemy.
Was he now off his head?

Well, when he knocked upon the door,
The servants cried as one,
'Get out of here this minute.
If we were you, we'd run,

'Or else 'twill be the worst for you.'
The 'beggar' stood his ground,
And said, 'Is great Aufidius
By any chance around?'

They couldn't quite believe his words.
They said, 'You've got a cheek.'
Before the 'beggar' could respond
They heard another speak.

'What can be going on in here?'
It was the 'beggar's' foe.
Aufidius, then entering, said,
'Come on, I want to know.'

He dressed in shabby garments

Coriolanus, in a tick,
Threw off his frayed disguise;
Aufidius, on seeing him
Could not believe his eyes.

'You're really pushing all your luck;
You're really not the one
Whom I'd have thought would venture here –
Not after all you've done.'

Coriolanus nodded,
'Yes,' he said, 'it's true;
I've caused distress and misery
And many pains to you.

'And if you wished to be revenged
For all the grief I've caused,
Well, here I am – do what you will.'
Then for effect he paused.

Then added, 'But if you should wish
To help me go back home,
I'll give you all the help I can
To go and conquer Rome.

'I'll be your loyal general –
You can rely on me –
And with the Volscian army
We'll set the Romans free.'

Aufidius was overcome –
But in a wink he said,
'We'll lead my army, arm in arm,
We'll both be at its head.'

Embracing Coriolanus,
He let emotions rule,
Forgetting their past warring ways...
You see, he was no fool.

He knew in Coriolanus
He had a partner who
Would simply be invaluable
In setting off to do

The things that would be needed
To win a victory,
Or, as his 'friend' had put it,
'Set shackled Romans free.'

But how the slippery world can turn,
How quickly things can change;
There is no doubt events can be
So fickle and so strange.

For back in Rome there's quarrelling:
The citizens have heard
Of the approaching Volscians,
And all that has occurred.

Of how great Coriolanus,
Who once was on their side,
Now heads this mighty army,
Its leader and its guide.

Menenius, in Rome, was heard
Most drily to observe,
'You threw our Coriolanus out –
It's what you all deserve.'

The Volscian camp as well displays
A change of attitude:
Aufidius now ponders –
He's in a jealous mood.

For he can see so clearly
That all the Volscian troops
Would die for Coriolanus,
For him they'd jump through hoops.

Their loyalty has now transferred,
As in a childish whim,
Unto the Roman general –
And now all lies with him.

So the respect and gratitude
That recently we saw
From bold Aufidius has dispelled –
It's shot right out the door.

He hates Coriolanus,
As he did in the past.
'I'll not forego revenge,' he vowed;
And thus the die was cast.

And so the Volscian army
Arrives before great Rome,
And Coriolanus coldly looks
At his once favoured home.

Menenius comes out to talk.
He says, 'Don't overrun
Your once beloved home, for you
Are still a Roman son.'

But Coriolanus won't undo
The things that he has done,
Simply to call it all a day –
Turn on his tail and run.

It won't make any difference
How much Menenius begs,
He won't scurry on his way
With tail between his legs.

But then quite unexpectedly
Some others come in view:
It is his wife and mother
Arriving out the blue.

And Coriolanus now can see
They've brought his little son.
The general ignores them all –
He seems intent to shun

The members of his family;
He doesn't want to hear
The things they have to tell him, or
Of their enormous fear.

Volumnia, his mother, cried,
Her voice borne down with gloom,
'Attacking your own land would be
Like treading on my womb.'

Coriolanus would not heed.
He turned to walk away;
Volumnia, however,
Had other words to say.

'If you destroy our city,
If you do wage this war,
Your name will be reviled and cursed
In Rome – for evermore.'

Coriolanus could no more
Resist his mother's pleas;
Her begging words and sorrow now
Had brought him to his knees.

He said he would withdraw, and that
He would no longer fight.
Aufidius then slyly said
That this was quite all right.

But to himself he archly thought,
'This could be good for me –
It shows a weakness I'll exploit.
I'll bide my time and see.'

Volumnia returned to Rome.
The crowd yelled out her name;
They saw her as their saviour
And met her with acclaim.

Meanwhile, Coriolanus leaves
And sullenly returns
To Antium with Aufidius,
Whose smouldering anger burns.

And he is quietly plotting
To kill his erstwhile friend.
He wants great Coriolanus
To quickly meet his end.

And so before a gathered throng
Of Volscians he now cries,
'Coriolanus was a coward.'
The general said, 'That's lies.'

Aufidius said, 'You yielded
To all your cowardly fears
The very moment that you saw
Your dear old mother's tears.'

Coriolanus shouted back;
They traded insults then –
Aufidius cried out for his death
And so did all his men.

The crowd of Volscians all joined in:
'Death to him – death we say!'
Coriolanus stood no chance;
Of fleeing on that day.

Aufidius and his faithful men
Drew swords and in a flash,
Aufidius cruelly struck him down –
There was an awful gash

Upon the former Consul's head;
He never could survive.
There was not now the slightest chance
That he could stay alive.

Some Volscian nobles there were shocked,
But yet Aufidius said,
'He could have been a danger –
It's better that he's dead.'

Aufidius cruelly struck him down

But then they gave Aufidius
Harsh words for what he'd done,
Then came to a decision
That suited everyone:

That Coriolanus' body should
Be buried there and then
With honour and the pageantry
Accorded to great men.

And when his rage and anger cooled
The bold Aufidius said,
'I now am struck with sorrow
To see my foe there dead.

'Though he created orphans
And widows in our land,
There never was a fighting man
More noble or more grand.

'So though he was our enemy
He'll be remembered here;
His boldness and his bravery
Will always be held dear.'

And there is grief and sadness
On everybody's face

HENRY THE SIXTH
Parts I, II and III

Henry the Fifth has sadly died,
His funeral's taking place,
And there is grief and sadness
On everybody's face.

For this King was dearly loved
While he had been alive,
And now to think he'd passed away
When only thirty-five.

It was the very saddest thing –
All stood before the cross
In great Westminster Abbey, there
To mourn their grievous loss.

The Duke of Bedford then proclaimed,
'This King was just so strong,
And noble, good and virtuous,
Too famous to live long.

'And England never lost a King –
The country ne'er gave birth,
To monarch quite so dearly loved,
A King of so much worth.'

But as this gracious noble speaks
Of everything he feels,
A messenger comes rushing in –
Before the Dukes he kneels.

And then he stands, erect and true,
The Dukes remain there seated;
He says, 'An English force in France,
Is cruelly defeated.

'Talbot, our commander bold,
Has lost the battle, so
He's now a prisoner of the French,
And also you should know

'The Earl Salisbury's now besieged
At Orleans, by mischance,
And finally the Dauphin, Charles,
Is crowned the King of France.'

The Duke of Bedford speaks out first.
'I'll not have this,' he cried.
'I'm going off to France right now,
Defeat, I'll not abide.'

The Duke of Gloucester spoke out too.
'I want to say one thing:
Henry the Fifth's small, infant boy
Must now be made our King.'

Meanwhile in France, Charles, now the King,
Has made another raid
On Orleans – but fails again;
And then he meets a maid!

His cousin Bastard says to him,
'Although things look so dark,
I think I have the remedy –
Her name is Joan of Arc.

'And so although your face looks sad,
For discord rules our land,
I say my Lord, be not dismayed
For succour is at hand.

'For here I bring this holy maid,
And though I risk derision,
I'm here to tell you that she's had
A quite amazing vision.

'It has come down from Heaven above
While she was in a trance,
And she's been told that she will drive
The English out of France.'

And so Charles said, 'Go call her in,
For I could use some aid.'
Bastard left and soon returned
Accompanied by the maid.

Now Joan was not the type to hide
Her light beneath a bush,
To get whatever she desired
She'd always shove and push.

She told the Dauphin, now the King
'I am the one you need
To send the English packing,
My sovereign Lord – take heed.

'Let me lead the army,
I promise then you'll find
That you will quickly be released
From all this awful bind.

'For I have seen a vision
From Heaven so I know
That I have been selected
To very boldly go

'And save Orleans for our side,
And you must have no doubt
It is my fate, now Henry's dead,
To drive the English out.'

Well Charles was very sceptical,
For she was but a maid,
But he was in a rotten fix
And very much afraid,

The English would defeat him –
He'd grasp at any straw
For France to be victorious
In this horrendous war.

He said, 'I am astounded
With all you've had to say
About this wondrous vision
You've shared with us today.

'But I say to be convinced –
To see what you can do –
I must in single combat
Now cross my sword with you.

'And if you vanquish me, I will
Believe your every word.'
Joan of Arc looked back at him
Quite calm and undeterred.

She chose her words most carefully,
'I am prepared, my Lord,
To fight to prove my words are true –
See here my keen-edged sword.'

Charles replied, 'I swear to God
No woman do I fear.'
And then he drew his sword and said,
'Now everyone, stand clear.'

They crossed their swords and Joan of Arc
Said, 'Thus I'll do or die,
For while I live, I say in truth
From no man will I fly.'

They fought until the King declared,
'A moment, stay thy hand.
You fight just like an Amazon
From some far, foreign land.'

The maid replied, 'I hope my King
You think me not a freak,
It is Christ's mother makes me strong,
Without her I'd be weak.'

The King replied, all business now,
'Whoe'er it is helps thee,
I little care, for I tell you,
'Tis you who must help me!'

And so a deal was quickly struck,
Joan said she would dispense
A thrashing to the English – then
Drive all the King's foes hence.

And she did all she promised,
For with sword and mace and lance,
She liberated Orleans town,
And won it back for France.

She liberated Orleans town

King Charles was mightily impressed.
'She is God's chosen one,'
He said; ''Tis Joan, not we, by whom
This day is surely won.'

But soon his pleasure turns to ire –
The English then attack,
And with great skill and bravery
Win Orleans right back!

Meanwhile back in England
The Earls are in dispute,
And squabbling over England's crown
Is at the quarrel's root.

Two factions now are forming;
There is much fighting talk
From Earls who are of Lancaster
And those who are of York.

The Duke of York puts out his hand
And picks a sweet white rose;
He gazes at it longingly,
Then holds it to his nose.

And so as all these different Earls
Placed flowers to their noses

'This rose shall be the symbol
Of our royal quest,' he said.
Vernon and Warwick copy him,
But others there pick red.

For Somerset and Suffolk
With eagerness then chose
For Henry's house of Lancaster
A glowing crimson rose.

And so as all these different Earls
Placed flowers to their noses,
Their actions gave the title to
The sad Wars of the Roses,

In which these two great houses
Contested for the throne;
Each was intent and quite resolved
To have it for his own.

And then against this background
Of ominous unrest,
Gloucester, the King's Protector, said,
'We're lucky, we've been blest

'With one who is a noble lad
To be our monarch – so
We'll travel now to Paris
And there with pomp and show

'We'll crown this worthy, little lad,
Henry the Sixth, he'll be.'
And with no more delay the court
Set out across the sea

To crown the little boy the King
Of France's noble realm.
He'd be the ruler of two states,
At France and England's helm.

For this was way back in the days
When English kings still claimed
A part of France within their realm,
When monarchs here were named

As King of France – and England too.
And so they planned with joy
A coronation for a King,
Though still a little boy.

The coronation over,
Attention now was turned
To fierce fighting with the French
Whose indignation burned.

Talbot, who has now been freed
(A ransom had been paid),
Fights the French outside Bordeaux,
And asks to have more aid.

His forces are outnumbered,
He doesn't stand a chance,
Without more help there is no doubt
A win will go to France.

Alas, no further troops are sent
And Talbot, with his son,
Fights with their men until they see
The French have truly won.

But Talbot's son, the brave young John
Refused to run away.
He said, 'I am resolved and set
That right here will I stay.

'For if I turn upon my tail
Before this fight is done,
I would be shamed for evermore
And not be Talbot's son.

'And so dear father, this I say,
I would much rather die,
Than leave the field with downcast head
And like a coward fly.'

Lord Talbot looked upon his son
And with a father's pride
He said, 'If you intend to fight,
Then I'll fight by your side.'

And so the father and the son,
Upon that dreadful day,
Took up their swords again to fight
Within that tangled fray.

They lost sight of each other – then
Lord Talbot took a wound –
Willing hands held him aloft,
They'd caught him as he swooned.

They laid him on the ground to rest,
And then some soldiers came,
They held a body steeped in blood –
They called John Talbot's name.

Lord Talbot lay there close to death,
Then hearing his son's name
He thought how awful fighting was –
That warring was no game.

For now the father realised
On seeing the blood shed,
That his adored, courageous boy –
His dear son, John, was dead.

'Oh, my poor boy,' he gasped aloud.
'Please lay him by my side
So I can wrap him in my arms.'
Oh, how Lord Talbot cried.

He shook with sheer emotion,
He said, 'Now all I crave
Is that my ancient arms can be
Poor young John Talbot's grave.'

They set the boy with care within
Lord Talbot's outstretched arm,
He wrapped his other round his son
As if to stave off harm,

In just the way he'd done before –
So many years ago,
When John had been a little boy,
Eyes bright and face aglow.

Lord Talbot said no further words,
There was no more to say,
And holding his beloved son
The sad Lord passed away.

Though England was defeated
It didn't take too long
For forces to re-gather
To right this tragic wrong.

And after further fighting
The English made their mark,
They captured as their prisoner
The French maid – Joan of Arc.

They took her to the English camp,
She begged them for her life,
But hatred for the wretched maid
By then was running rife.

The Duke of York insulted her
And though she was so young,
He called her hag and other things
And told her, 'Hold your tongue!'

But Joan replied and bravely.
She said, 'Do not make haste,
For I have lived a decent life,
Blameless, good and chaste.'

But York would hear no word of it,
He wanted retribution.
He cried, 'Enough, take her away!
See to her execution.'

She was sentenced right away,
They told her then and there
They'd tie her to a stake and burn
Her in the market square.

Then Warwick, he of kindly heart,
Said, 'I would like to make
A merciful attempt to ease
Her torture at the stake.

'Spare no faggots for the fire,
Let there be wood enough
So that her pain and suffering
Is short and not too tough.'

Joan then cried out most desperately –
Her words tore some apart –
'Will nothing have effect upon
Your unrelenting heart?

'For I am now with child,' she said.
'Don't send it to its doom;
This little baby lives right now
A child within my womb.'

The Duke cried out, 'Good heavens!
The holy maid with child!
It could be that the Dauphin has
Himself this lass defiled.

'But it will make no difference,
And it is all a lie;
Your pleadings will not save you
For you are doomed to die.'

'Then lead me hence,' the maid replied,
'For I will plead no more.'
They took her by each arm and led
The poor girl through the door.

As she left she laid a curse
With her last living breath:
'I hope your country suffers now
The gloomy shade of death.

'And may great mischief and despair
Within your land reside,
And drive you to the breaking point
And then to suicide.'

York answered her, 'Now be consumed
Into a pile of ash.
You are nothing, Joan of Arc,
You're just a piece of trash.

'For you are surely cursed and doomed
By some dread, awful spell,
And so be-gone – thou foul, accursèd
Minister of hell.'

And so they took her out to die,
They tied her to a stake,
And there they burned the maid to death,
But she left in her wake

A story that has stirred the souls
Of men through history,
Of how, though but a mere girl,
She tried to set France free.

Shortly after these events
The French King said, 'All right,
Let's call a truce and let's agree
We will no longer fight.'

Henry made him viceroy,
So everything was fine;
Their efforts, for the present,
The pair would now combine.

Meanwhile the Earl of Suffolk
Stood up and archly said,
'I think our new King Henry
Should now be getting wed.

They tied her to a stake

'And though he still is very young
I think that this young man
Should marry someone right away –
In fact, I have a plan.'

He said that Margaret of Anjou
Would be the one for him.
'She's very pretty in the face
And very lithe of limb.'

What he didn't say of course,
That sneaky, devious Earl,
Was that *he'd* had a little fling
With this fair, comely girl.

'If I can bring this off,' he thought,
'It could be good for me.'
So he was pleased when Henry said
He'd readily agree.

He'd gladly wed the lady,
She really looked first-rate,
She'd make a lovely wife and Queen,
She'd make a first-class mate.

The Earl was quietly overjoyed
To see this union flower,
He thought through young, sweet Margaret
He'd exercise all power.

'I'll rule young Margaret and the King
And thus control the realm;
Though no-one else will realise,
I shall be at the helm.

'The destiny of England
I'll hold – within my hand,
And it will be old Suffolk
Who rules this troubled land!'

So Suffolk travelled then to France,
He went without ado,
Just with the aim of bringing back
Young Margaret of Anjou.

He settled terms with her old dad
But on arriving back,
He found expressions on some Dukes
That looked extremely black.

They do not like what he's agreed
To cede to Margaret's dad;
Gloucester, Warwick, York as well,
All think the deal is bad.

For he has given at a stroke
Maine and Anjou too
Back to France – and all he's got
Is Margaret of Anjou.

Henry though is happy
For he really likes the look
Of her whom now he is to wed –
She's quite a lass to hook.

But he'd have been upset and hurt,
A most unhappy King,
If he'd had knowledge of the fact
That Suffolk's sneaky fling

Was still alive and carrying on,
For Suffolk was intent,
On keeping Margaret on a string –
On this he was hell-bent.

But anyway, the King is pleased
With all that's now in place;
He doesn't care he's given lands
When he sees Margaret's face.

The Duke of York is horrified,
The Earl of Warwick too;
They do not like the deal one bit
They hate it through and through.

Even the Duke of Gloucester
Who's Protector to the King
Thinks Suffolk has now gone and done
A really stupid thing.

And yet, despite his senior rôle,
Gloucester has much to fear;
The best advice for him is this,
'Be sure to watch your rear.'

For many hate the mighty Duke
As he is wont to boast
That he is closest to the King
All through his special post.

And there's a chance that he could be
The victim of attack.
Yes, Gloucester, if he's got good sense
Should really watch his back.

He has another problem too
That causes him some strife,
And that's his lady Duchess,
Sly Eleanor – his wife.

She is a rather silly sort
For she's inclined to preen,
And she informed him one fine day,
'I fancy being Queen.'

This sort of thing was typical
For it must now be said
That some at court had oft remarked
She had a swollen head.

The very Queen herself had cried
In anger, 'Look at her,
All done up in her finery
And wearing all that fur.

'Whoever does she think she is?'
And then the Queen would snort,
'She acts just like an empress
The way she comes to court.

'And strangers here, in truth, do think
When they at first have seen
Old Gloucester's daft, ambitious wife
That she's in fact the Queen.'

Now Gloucester often chided
His wife for her grand way,
But she would just ignore the words
The poor old Duke would say.

And so this was the state of things
When Henry said one day,
'Order Gloucester here at once,
Summon the Duke, I pray.'

The King was in St Albans
And Gloucester hurried there.
As he left his wife called out,
'I'll see you soon – take care.'

And once he'd gone, she hurried off
To carry out a scheme
That was as crazy as the look
That in her eye did gleam.

For now she took herself to see
A witch within her den.
She said, 'I've come to you to learn
The very latest gen

'On what the spirit will foretell,
So ask it now for me.
Will I become the Queen one day?
What will the future be?'

And so the awful, ugly witch
Called up a spirit then,
Who said, 'I've got some news right here
Concerning two proud men.'

And then her weak, old croaking voice
Said with a little groan,
'The King of England, Henry,
Will soon be overthrown.

'The King of England, Henry,
Will soon be overthrown'

'Also the Duke of Suffolk,
That mean and sneaky guy,
On water is now destined
To very shortly die.'

Eleanor gasped aloud at this
But ere she could say more,
There came a heavy pounding
Upon the witch's door.

Then York and Buckingham with guards
Came roughly bursting in,
And they told Eleanor with scorn
That what she did was sin.

And they arrested her and took
Her straight before the King,
Who shouted, 'You should really die
For this horrendous thing.

'Consulting with the witches
Is the worst thing one can do.
The penalty for this is death,
And this I'm sure you knew.

'But as you are most nobly born
I'll just impose a ban.'
And so he banished her that day
Unto the Isle of Man.

He said, 'Before you go, you'll walk
The streets of London town,
Where common folk can shout at you;
You'll wear a ragged gown.

'And this humiliation
Will entertain the crowd,
And make you cease for evermore
From being vain and proud.

'And as for you, Duke Gloucester,
I should really have you whipped,
But the title of Protector
Is from your shoulders stripped.

'And now I have no further wish
To look upon your face.'
So Gloucester left to contemplate
His fall and great disgrace.

Meanwhile the Duke of York
Speaks with a furrowed frown
To Salisbury and to Warwick,
They're all in London town.

He said, 'By rights, I should be King.'
He got into a lather.
'My family's rights were once usurped
By this young King's grandfather.

'When Bolingbroke assumed the crown
He stole my family's throne,
For it belonged by ancient right
To us and us alone.'

Warwick and Salisbury bent the knee
On hearing this bold talk.
'You are our rightful sovereign, sire,'
They tell the Duke of York.

York nods his head and slowly says,
'Yes, what you say is true,
But before I can be King
There's much for us to do.

'The white rose of the Yorkist cause,
Will now defeat,' he said,
'The blood red rose of Lancaster,
When its false King is dead.'

But news then came of trouble –
In Ireland it occurred –
And in no time, the Duke of York
Received the royal word

That he must travel there and quell
This latest discontent.
And so he quickly packed his bags
And that is where he went.

It was a timely act indeed –
Henry's command that day,
For at a stroke he got sly York
Quite safely out the way.

The King calls Gloucester back to him.
Alas, his only reason
Is so that Suffolk can arrest
The poor old Duke for treason.

They then led Gloucester from the room
And as he went he cried
To Henry and he warned the King,
'My Lord, watch every side,

'For you have foes on every flank.
They're bent on evil ends.
My Lord, remember what I say:
You don't have many friends.'

Queen Margaret says to Suffolk,
'I wish Duke Gloucester dead.
I'll only be relaxed for sure
When we've chopped off his head.'

She'd never liked the sad, old guy,
And now she thought, 'I may
Have my best chance to deal with him
And get him out the way.'

And so a little later on
Sly Suffolk came to say
The Duke of Gloucester had just then
Most sadly passed away.

King Henry turned quite white with shock
And cursed and loudly swore,
And then he fainted quite away
And fell onto the floor.

You see, Henry was kind-hearted,
Still had a soft spot for
Old Gloucester, even though the Duke
Was close to him no more.

When he came round he hit the roof;
He turned on Suffolk then
And said in no uncertain terms
He was the worst of men.

He blamed him for Duke Gloucester's death
But then the Queen jumped in;
She said to blame poor Suffolk there
Was really a bit thin.

But now Earl Warwick enters.
'Gloucester's dead,' he said.
'I think the Duke was strangled
As he lay upon his bed.

'His face was black and full of blood,
His eyeballs further out
Than ever in his life they were –
Of this I have no doubt.'

Henry lost his cool and said,
'All these foul deeds must halt.
And Suffolk, I blame you for this:
His death is all your fault.

'And so I banish you for good.
Don't ever come back here.'
The queen on hearing this, broke down,
And said she felt quite queer.

She cried, 'Oh, gentle Henry,
Let me plead for Suffolk there,
He's always been so good to you
And shown you every care.'

The King replied with flashing eyes,
Red faced and all a-froth.
'I tell you, if you plead for him,
'Twill just increase my wrath.

'And Suffolk, I do swear to you,
Despite my pleading wife,
If in three days you're in my realm,
Why then you'll lose your life.

'For if we find your worthless hide
Still lurking in our land,
The world itself won't ransom you
From death by axe-man's hand.'

Then he called, 'Come Warwick,
Good Warwick, come with me,
For I have matters of import
That I would share with thee.'

Now alone – the lovers there –
Earl Suffolk and the Queen,
Created such a woeful sight –
A most distressing scene.

The Queen cried, 'Let me take your hand
And cover it with tears.'
Suffolk took her in his arms
And tried to quell her fears.

She sighed, 'My Lord, when you depart,
You take my life as well.
Where will you go? How will you fare?
Wherever will you dwell?'

Suffolk replied, 'It matters not,
I really couldn't care,
For desolation rules supreme,
If you my dear aren't there.'

And so they made their last farewells.
The Queen said, 'Leave with me
Your loving heart, sweet Suffolk dear –
Take my poor heart with thee.'

And thus the lovers said goodbye,
A scene of bitter woe.
Suffolk turned and simply said,
'And now my Queen, I go.'

He left her there, bereft, alone,
And with no backward glance,
He headed off to banishment,
To cross the sea to France.

So Suffolk leaves the court and goes
From there to board a ship.
The last thing in the world he wants
Is thus to make a trip.

But exile's what he's got in store,
King Henry's had enough
Of all his scheming, lying ways –
At last he's acting tough.

But on the way to his new life
Earl Suffolk gets a shock.
He's captured by some pirates and
His head is on a block.

They tell him he's about to die.
Suffolk turns ghostly white,
And says, 'It's quite impossible,
It really isn't right,

'That I should die by menial hands
Of vassals such as you;
You're too low-born and horrible
For what you plan to do.

'A noble Lord like me should be
Dispatched by better folk.'
They laughed and said, 'We'll handle you
Like any other bloke.'

And so they chopped his head right off.
Then, being very mean,
They wrapped it up and sent it as
A present to the Queen.

And when the Queen received it
She got into a flap.
She cried out loud and vowed revenge
And hugged it to her lap.

She gasped, 'Here may his sweet head lie.'
She looked down on his face.
'But where's his noble body which
I should now here embrace?'

King Henry scowled with fearsome face –
'How now, my dear,' he said.
'Wouldst thou have mourned so much for me
If it were me there dead?'

The Queen was quick to answer.
'If you died, my love, you'd see
That I would never mourn for you,
For I would die 'twere thee.'

So we can see the Queen was smart,
Artful and all knowing.
In an instant she could see
The way the wind was blowing.

They wrapped it up and sent it as
A present to the Queen

Now things begin to gather pace.
The Duke of York returns
From Ireland and within his heart
A great ambition burns.

While he's been absent, he's had friends
Who've caused a great revolt;
It's really shaken Henry up
And given him a jolt.

For York has been hard at it –
He's done his very best,
To get a guy who's called Jack Cade
To stir up great unrest.

Cade's led a strong rebellion,
He's marched on London town.
He had the fervent aim in mind
To bring King Henry down.

The Duke of Buckingham, however,
Stopped him in his tracks,
And cut a deal to save the town
From any more attacks.

He pardoned everyone with Cade
If they would leave his cause.
He said, 'We cannot settle this
By having civil wars.'

So they'd abandoned poor Jack Cade
And he had taken flight,
But then he had been caught and killed
While on the run one night.

So this is how the kingdom stood
When York came back again,
And he was more determined that
He'd end King Henry's reign.

For this was now his time, he thought.
He'd grab the English throne,
For Henry only had the crown
On just a short-term loan.

He thought, 'I'll make the false demand
That if the King arrest
The Duke of Somerset – that man
Whom I so much detest.

'Well then, and only then, will I
Pull all my forces back.'
Of course, he hopes the King will say,
'Just do your worst – attack!'

He marched his troops on London,
Confident he'd teach
The King respect, and that the crown
Was now within his reach.

Buckingham rode to meet him,
And York said, 'If it's proved
That Somerset whom I detest
Is sacked and quite removed,

'Then, and only then, I'll stop
This march on London town,
And if he's sacked, I'll pledge myself
To Henry and the crown.'

This demand is mere pretence,
He hopes the King will say,
'The Duke of York can do his worst,
He shall not have his way.'

For this will give him reason
To carry on the fight;
He'd used the Duke of Somerset
To make his cause look right.

When York is told that Somerset
Is now no longer free
He has no option but to pledge
His total loyalty.

But then he hears from someone else
This claim is all untrue.
Somerset, whom he detests,
The man he would undo,

Is walking round as free as air...
And so the Duke then swore
That Henry's days were numbered.
He vowed, 'He'll reign no more.'

The armies then were both prepared,
And battle lines were drawn.
They met outside St Albans
Upon one early dawn.

King Henry's house of Lancaster
Opposed the Yorkists there,
To battle for the English throne,
To find out who would wear

The crown of England, who'd be King –
And so the fight began –
But it did not take long at all
Before the King's troops ran.

Henry fled to London,
And York with great delight
Said, 'What a massive victory!
We *did* put up a fight!

'But now we must proceed with haste
To good old London town,
And there kick Henry from the throne
And quickly claim the crown.'

The Duke of York is really sure
That this is now his hour,
And he takes steps right there and then
To seize all royal power.

But Henry soon comes on the scene,
And though things look quite bleak,
He acts as if he's still the King
And says, 'You've got a cheek.'

And then he really has a go –
He really has a moan;
He says to York, 'You'd better get
Your backside off my throne.'

York told him just to sling his hook.
He said, 'You need to know
I now am England's rightful King,
For you have had your go.

'It's now my turn to rule this land –
Look at the mess you've made.'
Henry replied with bold fine words,
Although a bit afraid,

'My title to the throne comes through
My dear old Grandad who
Was just as noble in his birth
And worthier far than you.

'Henry the Fourth, my Grandpapa,
A man of great renown,
A decent and fair-minded man,
By conquest won the crown.'

But as he spoke, King Henry
Well knew he partly lied,
And turning from the Duke of York
He said as an aside,

'I know my title's very weak
For Grandad stole the throne,
But that's a long way in the past;
We'll leave all that alone.'

But York's insistence he be King
Knocks Henry right off track,
And his resolve and stubbornness
Begin at last to crack.

For what he then proposes takes
All present by surprise:
He says, 'I'll tell you what we'll do
By way of compromise.

'I'll remain the King, but when
I've shuffled from this life,
When I am dead and live no more,
When free of all this strife;

'When I've laid down my burden
And said goodbye to care,
Well I do then propose, good York,
That you become my heir.

'And all your sons that follow you
Should also claim the crown.'
On hearing this, Queen Margaret's face
Took on a fearsome frown.

'How can you give away your throne?'
The Queen, distraught, bewails.
'How can you disinherit thus
Your son – the Prince of Wales?'

❧

The Duke of York has made his way
To Sandal Castle, where
His sons tell him he must resort
To bloody, bold warfare.

'It is the only way,' they say.
And then they tell him why.
'For you must be the country's King
Or be prepared to die.'

So war breaks out once more and now
The two great armies meet,
But after heavy fighting
York's forces all retreat.

The Duke of York is captured,
He's taken to the Queen,
I think we know already
That she's pretty tough and mean.

She laughs at him and harshly hurls
Great insults at the Duke,
But he was not the type to take
So vulgar a rebuke.

And though he was a prisoner
And at her mercy there,
He began to rage and fume,
To shout at her and swear.

Lord Clifford, too, was with the Queen
And he had cause to hate
The Duke of York, for Clifford's dad
Had sadly met the fate

Of early death when he'd been killed
Upon St Alban's field.
He'd fought against the Yorkists
And had refused to yield.

And so Lord Clifford blames the Duke.
He thinks that he's just bad.
He holds him guilty for the loss
Of his beloved dad.

And then Lord Clifford and the Queen
Both did an awful thing,
They leapt upon the Duke and stabbed
This man who would be King.

The Duke of York died painfully,
He fell down with a thud,
And lay there on the floor within
A pool of his own blood.

The Queen looked down at him and said
With monumental scorn,
'Take him to York and there behead
This traitor vilely born.

'And put it on a metal stake
And let the people gawk
At this foul creature rotting there,
This filthy son of York.'

'And put it on a metal stake'

303

The news of York's demise is brought
To two of his dear boys.
Edward and Richard hear with pain
Of all the Queen's foul ploys,

Of how she'd taunted their poor dad,
Of all that he'd been through,
And hearing this just made them vow
To gird their loins anew.

And then some more bad news arrives,
It tells of a defeat,
But says their other brother, George,
Is still intent to beat

King Henry and his forces –
And so he comes, this George,
With many troops from Burgundy
And now is set to forge

A path right through King Henry's force;
He's set on his endgame,
To bring poor Henry down and then
Enforce the Yorkist claim.

Meanwhile in York the Queen displays
The poor Duke's severed head.
King Henry there was mortified –
'Oh, awful deed!' he said.

But now York's sons have mobilised
Another army, so
They're set to have another try,
To have another go.

For they're determined that the Yorks
Will somehow gain the crown,
That Henry must receive at last
His overdue comedown.

And so another battle's fought.
This time the Yorkists win,
King Henry's forces all turn tail
And cry, 'We're giving in.'

So Henry too then fled the field
And as he did he said,
'I grieve to see these bodies here,
Sons, brothers, fathers – dead!'

And then he sees a boy bring in
His father whom he's killed,
And next a father brings his son
Whose blood he's also spilled.

And Henry there and then laments –
He's shaken to the core.
He hates relations fighting,
He loathes all civil war.

And so he turns his back and goes,
Leaves all the blood and gore,
And hopes that it will be the end
Of this infernal war.

As Henry left the field of blood
Lord Clifford was then found,
By Edward and young Richard,
Lying wounded on the ground.

'So what have we got here?' they say.
'Well, this is quite a prize!'
But as they taunt Lord Clifford
The wounded man there dies.

However, they still curse at him,
Although the poor man's dead.
And then as one they say, 'For Dad,
Let's cut off his foul head.'

So to avenge their father's death
They make Lord Clifford pay.
They take his severed head to York
And put it on display.

They then put plans in place to make
Edward, the first York King.
Richard and George gain titles too
That have a noble ring.

George gets the Duke of Clarence
And Richard, there and then,
Is made the Duke of Gloucester –
He's quite the worst of men,

For now he ponders to himself,
'How can I get the throne?
How many must I tread upon
To make the crown my own?'

Alone he contemplated
The spot on which he stood,
And said, 'I feel I'm standing
Within a thorny wood,

'From which I now must free myself;
I really can't relax,
Till I have hewn my way from here
With sharp and bloody axe.

'And nobody shall block my path
For if they do, I'll strike,
And all will feel my awful wrath,
Brother and foe alike.

'For I will murder anyone
With ruthlessness and guile,
And I can do all this with ease
And murder while I smile.'

It soon became apparent then
That he'd do anything
To push all others from his path
In order to be King.

What a villain! And I'm sure
He's one of whom you've heard,
For in the end this man became
King Richard, England's Third.

King Henry now is on the run,
He hides within a wood.
He's mumbling to himself and says,
'Margaret, my Queen, is good,

'For she has gone to Paris
To ask King Lewis there
If he will send some help to me
And heed this poor King's prayer.'

But as he's talking to himself
Two gamekeepers are near.
They're tramping through the forest...
One says, 'What's that I hear?'

They spot the King in hiding
And when they see him there
They recognise him instantly –
They'd know him anywhere.

They grab him and arrest him,
Take him within the hour
Before his enemies, who then
Confine him in the Tower.

Edward meanwhile is intent,
Beginning his new life,
To find himself a partner,
A rich and healthy wife.

His choice alights on Lady Grey.
His brothers tell him straight:
'She's not the person to be Queen,
For you she's no fit mate.'

But Edward's mind is quite made up.
He says, 'I'm set to marry,
And I can tell you one and all
I don't intend to tarry.'

The Earl of Warwick, who has played
A loyal helping hand
In making Edward England's King,
Now makes his own bold stand.

He doesn't like the news at all
Of Edward's plan to wed.
'I'll now support King Henry;
I'm changing sides,' he said.

And then he reached agreement
For his daughter, Lady Anne,
To marry Henry's worthy son,
A fine upstanding man.

This was the valiant Prince of Wales,
And so without delay
The two young people eagerly
Agreed their wedding day.

Then Warwick led his army on
A bloody, great onslaught;
He overpowered King Edward's troops,
And Edward then was caught.

And after they had locked him up
The Earl went straight away
To free King Henry from the Tower –
He went that very day.

So Henry was restored to power,
Became the King once more;
And he rejoiced in being King
The way he had before.

But while he was rejoicing
Upon this change of luck,
Some news came in that left him there
Amazed and quite dumbstruck.

For Richard, Duke of Gloucester,
Had sprung Edward from his jail,
And they had both escaped to France –
Poor Henry went quite pale.

And, truthfully, he had good cause,
For in no time at all
Edward and Richard had returned
For yet another brawl.

They came with massive forces
And marched on London town,
Even more determined
To seize the English crown.

They captured Henry once again,
And stripped him of his power,
And once more ignominiously
They threw him in the Tower.

It all comes to a head quite soon
When two great armies meet,
Advancing on each other,
Each praying they'll defeat

The other side with little loss.
They're both intent to win,
For neither side has any thought
Of ever giving in.

Queen Margaret leads King Henry's troops,
Set to defend his realm;
The other's led by Edward –
He rides there at its helm.

The armies clash on Tewkesbury field
And, after a great fight,
Edward's forces win the day,
Margaret's all take flight.

Queen Margaret is captured then;
The Prince of Wales is too.
Edward says to Wales, 'Good sir,
What shall we do with you?'

The Prince of Wales is young and brave;
He calls his captors names,
He mocks all Edward's 'fancy' plans,
Derides his regal claims.

'Lascivious Ed!' he calls him.
Richard – 'Misshapen Dick.'
He said, 'You and your brothers
Make me and my dad sick.'

The brothers wouldn't stand for this.
They said, 'Now watch your tongue.
We won't take cheeky talk like that
From someone who's so young.'

But the Prince of Wales was brash,
He let his insults fly,
So Edward and his brother there
Decided he must die.

And thus without another word,
Richard, and Edward too,
Leapt forward, both declaring,
'We now will silence you.'

Right there before his mother
These two grim Yorkist males
Both stabbed King Henry's much loved son,
They killed the Prince of Wales.

Then, Richard, Duke of Gloucester
Right on that very hour,
Jumped on his horse and rode all night
To London and the Tower.

He made his way to Henry's cell,
Within those thick, grey walls.
It's there the final act of hate
'Twixt these two sides befalls.

Gloucester told the jailor, 'Go!
Leave us alone, good sir.
It is essential that you leave
For we must now confer.'

'So flies the restless shepherd
From the wolf,' King Henry cried.
'Suspicion haunts the guilty mind,'
The evil Gloucester sighed.

'You've come to kill me,' Henry breathed.
Richard of Gloucester said,
'You think I wish your swift demise,
Just like your son who's dead.'

Henry groaned as he dwelt on
His son, of so much worth.
He cried, 'An owl shrieked out upon
The moment of your birth.

'And dogs howled then – a tempest shook
The trees and pulled them down,
And ravens croaked on chimney pots
In every English town.

'For you were born with many teeth
And this did signify,
You came into the world to bite
And cause good folk to die.

'You are a foul, ungodly sight,'
King Henry spoke with scorn.
'Thousands will come to rue the day
This Yorkist cur was born.'

This insult Richard quite ignores
And swiftly draws his knife;
Then with a treacherous, fatal thrust
He takes King Henry's life.

As Henry drew his final breath
He sank onto one knee
And cried, 'O God, forgive my sins –
Gloucester, I pardon thee.'

Then he collapsed upon the floor –
Said Gloucester with a sigh,
'King Henry and his son are gone
But now some more must die.

Then with a treacherous, fatal thrust
He takes King Henry's life

316

'For I would have the throne and so
Some kin must die as well.'
Without a doubt, this Yorkist Lord
Was like a fiend from Hell.

And with this act of murder
Our sorry tale now closes.
It drops the final curtain on
The sad Wars of the Roses.

For Edward now was free to rule;
He'd won through everything
And now became Edward the Fourth
To reign as England's King;

But if you wish to find out more
Of all that then occurred
You'll have to read the story of
King Richard, England's third.

He now returned in triumph

TITUS ANDRONICUS

Titus Andronicus,
A general of Rome,
After years of fighting wars
Finally came home.

He'd been away for ages
Engaged in a great cause,
Battling with the fearsome Goths
In many bloody wars.

He now returned in triumph,
Having earned such fame
That every Roman citizen
Was yelling out his name.

And he'd brought home some hostages,
Amongst them Goth's fair Queen,
Who was as easy on the eye
As any woman seen.

Her name was Queen Tamora
And she's a captive there,
And Titus is about to add
To this fair Queen's despair.

For she has her three sons with her
And holds each one so dear,
But she is worried for their fate –
Her mind is filled with fear.

And with good cause and reason
It must be truly said,
For Titus then declared with force,
'I grieve some sons, who're dead.

'And they will only rest in peace
And go to paradise,
If I give succour to the gods
With human sacrifice.'

Then turning to Alarbus,
Tamora's first-born son,
'Someone must die,' he coldly said,
'And you shall be the one.'

Tamora was beside herself
She pleaded for her child,
She fell upon her knees and cried,
She really went quite wild.

But it did not an ounce of good,
No matter what she said:
Alarbus had been chosen
So he was good as dead.

They led the poor young lad away,
A soldier drew his knife,
And in a tick they finished off
Alarbus's short life.

Tamora made a silent vow
That she would get revenge,
She whispered quietly to herself;
'My son – I will avenge.

'And I'll not rest a moment now
Till Titus pays for this.'
Thus she spoke, her eyes ablaze,
Her voice a soulless hiss.

Then Titus' brother, Marcus, said,
'The crowd all love you so,
Perhaps you should be Emperor.'
But Titus just said, 'No!'

And he was really adamant;
He turned the offer down,
And said that Saturninus
Should wear the Roman crown.

Saturninus was the son
Of the Emperor who'd died,
And when he heard what Titus said,
Replied, 'I'll make my bride

'Your daughter, fair Lavinia –
I'll take her for my wife,
And then our two great families
Will be entwined for life.'

Now this seemed very neat indeed,
A really great conclusion –
But for you to think this so
Would simply be delusion.

For she had been betrothed awhile
To Saturninus' brother,
And she had made it very clear
She didn't want another.

And so when the new Emperor
Stood up and boldly said,
'Yes, I will have Lavinia,
The two of us shall wed',

His brother, Bassianus,
And good Lavinia both
Reminded Saturninus
That they had pledged their troth.

The general was angry
To see his daughter try
To shun great Saturninus –
How did she dare defy

The man who was the Emperor!
And so he tried to seize
His daughter and bring her to heel –
He just ignored her pleas.

But Titus's son, Mutius
Stood in his father's way;
Titus went ballistic –
'Don't mess with me today.'

Then angry Titus in his rage,
Ignoring everyone,
Turned around and calmly killed
Mutius – his son.

And then he told Lavinia,
'After this swift slaughter
I think you'll wed the Emperor now –
You will obey, my daughter.'

But Emperors can be fickle –
They have a roving eye –
For when great Saturninus
Did at first espy

The lovely Queen Tamora,
Well, you know how it is,
In but a moment he resolved
To make the fair Queen his.

So Saturninus was intent
Upon this other wish,
For Tamora seemed to be
A much more tasty dish.

He now refused Lavinia.
'Tamora's who I'll wed,
And as I am the Emperor
I'll have my way,' he said.

And so it was they married,
But we must here record
As Titus knelt before them both
There still was much discord.

For though Tamora spoke and said,
'Good Titus, rise, I pray.'
Beneath her breath she slyly had
Some different words to say.

She whispered to her husband:
'In time, my Lord, I'll find
A way to murder them – they are,
A curse to all mankind.'

She meant, of course, bold Titus,
His sons and daughter too;
She swore she'd have complete revenge
For what he'd put her through.

But now it turns quite nasty.
In fairness, I should say,
If you are tender-hearted,
You'll want to turn away.

Tamora had a lover,
And Aaron was his name –
He was a Moor and revelled in
Her sudden rise to fame.

He knows that she still loves him,
So everything is fine,
For though she's now the Empress
He's sure, 'She still is mine'.

For he had been her lover
Back in her lost Goth home,
Before they had been captured
And dragged by force to Rome.

And though she is now married
To the Emperor – he's sure
She will remain his own sweet love,
Now and for evermore.

Tamora had two other sons –
This you already knew –
Both yearned for fair Lavinia,
Both were keen to woo.

Tamora had a lover,
And Aaron was his name

They spoke to Aaron of their wish –
'To court a Roman's daughter
Is something that I know,' he said,
'Will land you in hot water.'

The lads, however, laughed at him.
One son, Demetrius, told
How he could handle anything
That Fortune might unfold.

His brother Chiron felt the same,
So Aaron told them how
The boys could have their way with her,
How they could get it now.

'Fine ladies to the woodland go
To shun the heat of day,
So pounce upon this woman there
And have your wicked way.

'There is no need for fancy words,
Just take the maid by force.'
And thus it was that these two rogues
Were set upon their course.

We enter now upon a scene
Within a shady wood
Where we find Aaron, mean and bad –
This man is just no good.

And then Tamora joins him there,
She says with artful smile,
'You have been on my mind, sweet love.
Shall we romance awhile?'

But Aaron shook his head and said,
'I do not feel inclined
For I have other things right now
That occupy my mind.'

Then Bassianus, as he spoke
Came walking into view.
Lavinia was there as well,
They said, 'How do you do?'

But soon an argument breaks out
Between the rival pair.
It gets extremely heated
As they all argue there.

Then Chiron and Demetrius
Appeared upon the scene;
Tamora railed about the way
Lavinia had been.

She told her two devoted sons,
'Lavinia called me "foul",
And Bassianus too was rude.'
The lads began to scowl.

'We will take revenge for you,'
The awful pair then cried.
'This Bassianus lives too long –
It's time the fellow died.'

They grabbed the Emperor's brother.
What could Bassianus do?
He really didn't stand a chance
When set upon by two.

They murdered Bassianus,
They struck the poor man down –
And with Tamora's blessing
For she now wore the crown,

And she could do what e'er she wished,
And what she wished to do
Was be revenged on Titus
And all his family too.

She turned towards her selfish sons,
Her face was wracked with pain.
She said, 'Do you remember boys
How I cried tears in vain,

'To save your brother from his fate?
He paid an awful price,
When Titus made my lovely boy
A human sacrifice.

'So take Lavinia, do your worst.'
Her voice was high and shrill.
'Away with her, exact revenge –
Just use her as you will.'

Lavinia pleaded desperately,
'Have mercy please, I pray.'
Tamora's sons just laughed out loud,
Then dragged the girl away.

Poor Lavinia cried in shock,
For she was so afraid,
And with good cause, for they were set
On raping the poor maid.

The corpse of Bassianus
They threw into a pit...
And now I must give warning
Of another awful bit.

The younger sons of Titus,
Quintus and Martius too,
Are lured by Aaron to this pit;
The pair just have no clue,

They fall into the hole

331

That they are in great danger –
They fall into the hole.
To make them seem like murderers
Was evil Aaron's goal.

For with great care and cleverness
The ghastly Aaron built
A story that would make quite sure
That every ounce of guilt

Was placed on Titus's two sons:
He told the Emperor how
Good Bassianus had been slain
By both of them, just now.

When Titus heard, he was distraught;
In shock he felt quite numb.
But he could not have dreamt at all
That worse than this would come.

His brother Marcus found his girl,
Lavinia, sweet and fair,
Alone and walking silently
With mad and vacant stare.

For Chiron and Demetrius,
Tamora's frightful sons,
Had carried out a monstrous act
That everybody shuns.

They'd raped the precious innocent,
So maidenly and young,
And so she couldn't tell on them
They had ripped out her tongue.

And they had cut her hands off too –
To tell it makes one pale;
It was a really ghastly thing...
This is a vicious tale.

Marcus took her in his arms;
He held his trembling niece,
He tried his best to comfort her
And make her shaking cease.

He knew he had to do one thing –
Take her to Titus – so
He headed for his brother's house
He had to let him know

Exactly what had happened.
But what would Titus do?
What would his reaction be
When once the poor man knew?

Now Quintus and young Martius had
Been pulled out from the hole –
Accusing them of murder
Was evil Aaron's goal.

So Titus stood there pleading,
'Spare my dear sons,' he cried.
'I know my boys are innocent,
Somebody must have lied.'

But no-one there was listening
To Titus's wild pleas,
Their attitude made him distraught
And very ill at ease.

But then into the judgement hall
His brother Marcus came,
And with him came an atmosphere
Of fearful gloom and shame.

For with him was Lavinia,
A devastating sight.
Poor Titus just collapsed and sobbed
To see his daughter's plight.

And when she heard her brothers
Were facing their demise,
All saw the tears of sadness
Well up in her blue eyes.

When Titus saw this happen
It really was too much –
She could no longer speak a word,
She'd lost her sense of touch,

And yet she fretted for her brothers.
What a noble child!
To think she thought of them, although
She had been so defiled.

He scooped her up into his arms,
This ill-used child of Rome,
And holding all his pain inside
He took his daughter home.

It was a most distressing time
Of dreadful family woe;
And then into this shocking scene
Arrived a foe we know.

Aaron entered with some news –
He from the palace came.
Saturninus sent the rogue;
He acted in his name.

The news was that the brothers
Who both now stood accused
Of murdering Bassianus
Could maybe be excused.

They might receive a pardon,
And get off being tried,
But there was one condition
That must not be denied.

The family Andronicus
Must find someone to give
One of their hands, if they should wish
For these two lads to live.

Titus and his oldest son –
Lucius he was named –
Conferred with Marcus as to who
Should end up being maimed.

All three of course were quite prepared
To make the sacrifice,
Each had agreed to lose a hand,
They all would pay the price

If it would mean the liberty
Of Titus's two lads;
But Titus thought, this was for sure
A duty just for dads.

And so he tricked the others
Into leaving him, just so
That he could make the sacrifice
And thus appease their foe.

He turned to wicked Aaron
And bent his weary head.
'Take up your knife and do the deed –
Sever my hand,' he said.

Aaron didn't hesitate –
He cut through flesh and bone.
Titus stood there stoically,
He didn't even groan.

Then Aaron made a promise
That he would soon return,
'And I shall bring your sons with me.'
Titus did not discern

The lying look upon his face,
He didn't hear him say,
'Their heads, I mean – that's what I'll bring,
Laid out upon a tray.'

And he was truthful to his word
For when he reached the court,
He gave the Emperor the hand,
And then the sons were brought

From out of prison in their chains.
Their pleas were all refuted,
And they were swiftly taken out –
And both were executed.

A messenger then took the hand
And both the severed heads
To Titus, who just thought his life
Was torn in little shreds.

But he dispatched bold Lucius
And made a solemn vow:
'I promise that we'll have revenge.
Go raise an army – now!'

Then he and Marcus took the heads
To bury them somewhere –
Lavinia took the severed hand
And carried it with care.

She held it firmly with her teeth
Despite her dreadful plight.
What a truly awful scene –
What a gruesome sight.

A messenger then took the hand
And both the severed heads

Later Titus sat beside
His poor, maimed little girl;
He'd very nearly lost his wits,
His mind was in a whirl.

But brave Lavinia was intent
On showing Titus who
Had done these awful things to her –
She felt that if he knew

He'd certainly take action
Against the evil pair.
And so with looks and gestures
And pointing here and there

She made her father understand
Just who the culprits were,
And Titus made it clear to all
He'd seek revenge for her.

He had a message then engraved
Upon a small brass plate,
Which message clearly advertised
His overpowering hate.

It also made it very plain
He knew who'd raped his girl.
Whoever read the message
Would see the truth unfurl.

He sent the plate to Chiron
And to Demetrius too;
He wanted this appalling pair
To find out that he knew.

But when they read the message
They mocked it to the hilt,
Though Aaron who was standing there
Saw Titus knew their guilt.

Meanwhile at the palace
Tamora's given birth:
A new son for the Emperor,
A child who should be worth

A king's own ransom to the realm.
But there's a mystery here:
The child is of a dusky hue –
Now that is really queer.

He is not the Emperor's boy,
He's Aaron's babe, and so
It really is imperative
The Emperor doesn't know.

So Aaron hatches out a plan
Whereby he'll institute
A scheme to place a fair-haired boy
To be a substitute.

When Aaron looked upon his child
He felt a father's awe;
He called him 'beauteous blossom',
A bonny lad for sure.

'The child must live,' the Moor declared.
'The truth must not be found.
I'll take him to the Goths to live;
They'll keep him safe and sound.'

So no-one there would know his scheme
He did a thing much worse
Than anything he'd done before:
He killed Tamora's nurse.

He slew the midwife there as well,
She also lost her life,
So Saturninus would not know
He had a faithless wife!

And so with that he left the court
And sad Tamora there,
To take his infant to the Goths
And place him in their care.

When Saturninus heard the news
That Lucius made way
With all the army of the Goths,
He had these words to say:

'The Roman people much prefer
Young Lucius to me.'
Tamora said, 'Don't worry, Lord.
I'll sort it out, you'll see.'

She said, 'I'll make this Titus,
Who I think is mad with pain,
Persuade his son, young Lucius,
To see good sense again.

'I'll get him to convince his son
To join with us once more,
To cease his siding with the Goths –
Not start another war.'

Then later on the scheming Moor
Was captured by a Goth
Who took him to bold Lucius,
To there confront his wrath.

Aaron had his little boy
Tucked safely in his arm,
A tiny lad, whom you'd have thought
No-one would want to harm.

But Lucius gave the order
For both of them to die...
When Aaron heard this sentence
He gave an anguished cry.

'If you will spare my little son
I'll tell you everything.'
Lucius thought his frightened words
Betrayed a truthful ring.

And so he listened quietly
As Aaron spoke with speed
About the nasty things he'd done,
And every dreadful deed;

Of how he'd done his very best
To cause a load of strife
For Titus and his family
And quite mess up his life.

Of every loathsome action –
Of every nasty ploy –
And then he said Tamora was
The mother of his boy.

He said her sons had been the ones
Who had so cruelly slain
Bassianus – then he told
How he had set in train

The raping of Lavinia –
Of what he'd said that day,
To urge Tamora's frightful sons
To carry on that way.

He told Lucius of his hate,
Of how he wished to see
Unhappiness brought down upon
The general's family.

Lucius asked, 'Do you regret
The awful things you've done?'
Aaron scoffed and he replied,
'No, not a single one!'

When he'd finished, Lucius said,
'He really must not die
A death as sweet as hanging –
It's too good for this guy.'

But despite these sombre words
Lucius said that he
Would heed foul Aaron's last request,
The frantic father's plea,

And spare the lovely little boy,
He would grant Aaron's prayer
For his beloved son to live
And to be placed in care.

Tamora, meanwhile, reached a pact
For Titus to arrange
A meeting 'twixt the Emperor
And Lucius – to exchange

Their views on all the problems,
A chance for them to see
If they could sort the whole mess out
And somehow could agree.

But prior to the meeting,
Titus, the cunning chap,
Set out to lure Tamora's sons
Into a devilish trap.

And once they are within his grasp,
Once they're within his sphere,
He strings them up and slits their throats,
He cuts them ear to ear.

Then Lucius, his son, arrives,
Tamora comes as well,
With husband Saturninus –
Now comes a scene from hell.

For Titus serves them both a meal,
A tasty-looking pie,
But it is such a ghastly thing –
You may well wonder why.

Well, it contained the severed heads
Of those two horrid boys
Who'd treated sweet Lavinia
Just like a box of toys.

And so Tamora and her spouse
Sat down to eat a meal
Of those two sons she loved so much –
She thought she'd eaten veal!

Then to the Emperor, Titus spoke
'My Lord, do you recall
The story of Virginius,
And all that did befall?

'He slew his girl when she was raped,
He killed to save her shame,
He did it so that he could then
Recover his good name.

A tasty looking pie

'And so my Lord, please will you tell –
My Lord, I beg of you –
Was this a right and proper thing
For this poor man to do?'

The Emperor declared it was:
'He really had no choice.'
Titus said, 'Well here's my girl
Who has no hands or voice...

'And she was raped and so I say
Most humbly, Lord, to you,
To save my family's honour
She must be murdered too.'

And then in front of all of them
His darling girl he slew.
'Now with thy shame, my sorrow dies;
It's what I had to do.'

Saturninus then cried out,
'Hold! Everyone take heed.
I want the culprits brought at once
Who did this awful deed.

'Those who defiled Lavinia,
Bring them here I say.
Who was it did this loathsome thing?
Can someone tell, I pray?'

Said Titus, ''Twas Demitrius
And wicked Chiron too.'
The Emperor cried, 'Oh what a thing
For these two boys to do.'

Titus said, 'These wretched curs
Both deserved to die,
And that is why I killed them both
And baked them in this pie.'

Tamora screamed out loud to hear
Such dreadful, ghoulish news.
Her hatred for bold Titus
Had caused her now to lose

The two sons whom she idolised;
She just could not conceive
She'd eaten them – but Titus gave
Her no more time to grieve.

For hastily he crossed the room
And taking out a knife
He thrust it at the Empress
And took Tamora's life.

Saturninus then jumped up,
He also held a knife,
He was determined to avenge
The murder of his wife.

He killed poor Titus in a flash –
Another body fell;
But that was not the end of it,
There is still more to tell.

For Lucius then deftly struck
The Emperor such a blow
That laid him with the other dead –
Four bodies in a row.

It was a scene of misery,
Of death and blood and gore;
But happily I now can say
There isn't too much more.

For Lucius was made Emperor –
A good choice you could say;
But then he was the only one
That still survived that day.

The others who could fill the post
Lay dead upon the floor;
But Lucius was a decent choice
Who would uphold the law.

And, using Roman principles,
The first thing that he did
Was to proclaim to all the world,
'Behold! We shall be rid,

'Of this horrendous Aaron:
One thing I surely vow,
He will die a lingering death,
So take the scoundrel now.

'And bury him up to his neck
Out in the summer heat,
And don't let anybody dare
To give him food to eat.

'And let him die by inches
Until his final breath.
For never lived a rogue who more
Deserved this painful death.'

So wicked Aaron paid the price,
Alone without a friend,
Though he was unrepentant,
Right to the very end.

Lucius ordered funerals
For the others who had died.
'But not for foul Tamora,'
The brand new Emperor cried.

'She's denied all honours,
So heed now what I say,
Throw her remains out to the dogs
And to the birds of prey.'

The Emperor's wishes were fulfilled.
They settled down once more
With everyone determined now
To live within the law.

So as we close this bloody tale,
This quite appalling tome,
We can but hope that Lucius
Will bring some peace to Rome!

They're fighting every single day

354

TROILUS AND CRESSIDA

War is such an awful thing,
So many people die,
And often soldiers can't recall,
They can't remember why,

They're fighting every single day,
What they are battling for,
What started it at first – indeed,
The reason for the war.

Thus it was outside of Troy:
Greek soldiers all had tramped
To Troy – and there for seven years,
Their forces had encamped.

For all these years they had fought on –
Attack and then attack –
And as the Greeks besieged poor Troy,
The Trojans fought on back.

Whatever was the reason
For this protracted war?
Why were the Greeks so thus intent –
What were they fighting for?

Well, Priam who was King of Troy
Had three sons he adored;
They were brave and bold and brash
And all could use a sword.

The oldest was called Hector,
Paris was another,
And Troilus, who loved Cressida,
He was the youngest brother.

Now seven weary years before,
Paris of Troy had done
A deed that Greeks both near and far,
In fact just everyone,

Believed to be the meanest act.
This selfish, horrid boy
Had stolen beauteous Helen and
Had taken her to Troy.

She was the wife of Menelaus,
King of Sparta, so
It's not surprising that the Greeks
Made up their minds to go

To Troy and there besiege the town –
The actions of the lad
Had got the Greeks in angry mood;
Oh, they were really mad.

And so the Greeks had come to Troy
Intent to get her back;
And this then was the reason
For this seven-year attack.

Now Troilus was the brother
Of naughty Paris there,
And he is desperately in love
With Cressida, so fair.

He says, 'I'm sick of fighting,
I want to take a wife,
I want to settle down and start
To live a normal life.

'I'm tired of living in a place
Where only fighting rules,
As far as I'm concerned they're all
A bunch of silly fools.'

So he decides he'll have a bash
To win the maiden's hand.
He wants to give the lovely girl
A shiny wedding band.

But in these ancient days of yore
It wasn't the done thing
To tell a girl, 'I fancy you.
Hey, wear my wedding ring.'

It happened in a special way –
For if a youth was keen,
His courting was done for him by
A trusted go-between.

And so he asked his uncle –
Pandarus was his name –
If he would go and carry out
The age-old wooing game.

'Tell her how much I love her,
That she's the one for me.'
His uncle said, 'Don't worry, lad.
I'll sort it out, you'll see.'

So Pandarus then made his way
To Cressida right there,
And said, 'My nephew Troilus
Will wither in despair,

'If you refuse to love him,
If you deny his suit.'
For a moment Pandarus
Thought he would get the boot.

She looked down her nose at him,
Looked cool and very coy,
And said she thought young Troilus
Was just a silly boy.

But then with more persuasion
She blurted out the truth,
And said she thought that Troilus
Was quite a handsome youth.

And then she came right out with it
And said, 'I must tell you
His true love isn't wasted,
For I love Troilus too.'

'Then come along,' said Pandarus,
'To Troilus right away.'
And she spent loving time with him
For all of that long day.

And they professed their passion:
They each said, 'I love you.'
And you would think you could be sure
That they would both be true!

The Greeks who're camped outside the walls
Are sitting down to sup,
And almost every one of them
Is feeling quite fed up.

And almost every one of them
Is feeling quite fed up

They've had enough of this long war.
And Ulysses then says,
'We've been here far too long, you know –
More than two thousand days.'

And there within the city,
Behind the walls of Troy,
They're fed up with it all as well –
There isn't too much joy.

'What the heck!' then Hector says.
'Helen has caused such woe.
Let's give her to the Greeks – just let
The silly woman go.

'She's not worth all this trouble,
She's caused us so much pain,
Let's give her back and then enjoy
Some peace here once again.'

But Troilus then spoke up and said,
'But what about those slain?
If we just give her back it means
That they all died in vain.'

And so they argued back and forth
With no conclusion made.
They didn't give fair Helen back
But made another trade.

For Cressida is just about
To find her life turned round.
And all her plans for marriage
Are soon to run aground.

For she, who'd thought she'd surely be
A bride in just short weeks,
Now finds her father wishes her
To join him with the Greeks.

For he'd gone over to their side
Many years before,
And now he wants his daughter back,
To be with him once more.

A deal is very quickly done:
The Greeks agree to trade
A prisoner for Cressida –
And thus a deal was made.

And so the Greeks then send a lad
To bring the young girl back.
He makes his way to Troy's great walls
Along a little track.

Diomedes was this lad's name,
A brave guy through and through.
Muscular and full of charm
And so good looking too.

Cressida says fond farewells
To Troilus standing there;
With tears welling in her eyes
She cries, 'I'll always care.

'There'll never be another love
In all my life but you,
And when I'm taken far away
I'll not know what to do.'

And so with tender kisses
The two young lovers part,
And vow the other always
Will own their loving heart.

And Troilus there and then avows,
'Somehow I'll find a way
To creep into the Grecian camp
And see you every day.'

The lovelorn lass now makes her way,
With the young, handsome lad,
Back to the Greek encampment
To be with her old dad.

And as she follows this young man
The girl begins to feel
That Troilus whom she's left behind
Is really no big deal.

In fact she thinks, 'I like this lad.'
Oh, what a fickle wench!
We all thought leaving Troilus
Had been a massive wrench.

※

But now Prince Hector, who's a champ,
The finest fighter there,
Decides it would be jolly good
To set the Greeks a dare.

He challenges just any Greek
To come against his might.
He says, 'Has any soldier there
Still got the nerve to fight?'

He thinks they'll send Achilles,
A fighter bold and cruel,
But this warrior's not inclined
To get into a duel.

He's Greece's greatest warrior,
In battle, such a sight,
But at this time he's sulking and
Won't leave his tent to fight.

He says, 'Has any soldier there
Still got the nerve to fight?'

His problem is that he is full
Of silly, childish pride.
He thinks he's not revered enough –
So in his tent does hide.

And so the Greeks send Ajax;
But these two were related,
And thus they found their fighting urge
Had very soon abated.

Hector cried, 'Let's have a truce.
We shouldn't fight each other.
After all you're close enough
Almost to be my brother.'

And so the Greeks and Trojans too
Agreed a truce that night,
But on the 'morrow all agreed
They would resume the fight.

So they sat down to celebrate –
The Greeks and Trojans, all.
It really was the strangest thing;
They really had a ball.

Achilles had now changed his mind
For he was quite hell-bent
On fighting – and so now he asked,
Bold Hector to his tent.

He wished to size the Trojan up –
He was intent to know
If Hector really was the type
To make a worthy foe.

He told his good friend Patroclus,
'I'll heat his blood tonight
With Grecian wine – tomorrow though
I'll cool it in a fight.'

Now Troilus who was also there,
Said, 'I'll now go and seek
For my beloved Cressida.'
The thought made him feel weak.

And so he went a-searching,
And to his horror saw
His lover with the young Greek lad.
He cried out, 'Oh, you whore!

'Oh Cressida! Oh Cressida!
How could you be untrue!'
But the damage had been done
And this poor Troilus knew.

He vowed that when the fighting
Resumed the following day
He'd kill the fawning Grecian lad;
He'd kill him in the fray.

The next day when the sun appeared
And dawn burst through once more.
The Trojans and the Greeks again
Returned to bloody war.

True to his word, then Troilus
Sought Diomedes out.
They both fought hard – a stirring sight
Of that there was no doubt.

But neither gained the upper hand.
There really was no way
That either would claim victory
On that particular day.

Then in the heat of battle
Achilles and Hector met,
The stage for a great struggle
Was well and truly set.

But after a quite short exchange
Of thrusts and blows and all,
Achilles, puffing hard, exclaimed,
'I'm too tired out to brawl.

'So let me take a breather,
I'm really out of shape.'
And Hector his opponent then
Just let the Greek escape.

He could have overpowered him.
He could have won the day.
But Hector let Achilles go –
An act of great fair play.

Hector continued fighting,
His sword flew all around,
And many Grecian soldiers
He struck down to the ground.

And through that raging, crashing throng
Hector delivered death,
Until he said, 'My work is done.
I'll now regain my breath.

'My sword has had its fill today
Of blood and death and gore,
So for today I'll say "Enough",
And I will fight no more.'

But as he laid his sword aside,
Thus totally unarmed,
And certain in the knowledge that
He would remain unharmed,

Achilles came back on the scene.
He had a band of men –
His Myrmidons, his warriors –
He turned around and then,

Ignoring rules of chivalry,
Cried, 'Slaughter Hector here!'
And that is what they did; they killed
This man who knew no fear.

Then Achilles set about
A really awful thing.
A quite disgraceful act upon
The son of Troy's great King.

He tied the bleeding body
Of Hector, to his horse,
Then jumped astride his weary steed
And then he set his course

Towards the massive walls of Troy,
And there he showed them all
How he had slain their much loved Prince,
And what would thus befall

Those who opposed Achilles –
There'd be a price to pay.
The Trojans to a man were stunned
By all they saw that day

And for a moment some declared,
'Let this now end the war.'
But Troilus up and said he felt,
That he was really sure,

That Hector's death should be avenged;
They couldn't let it go.
It was a coward's act, performed
By an unworthy foe.

So the fighting recommenced...
A moral's here for sure:
That violence begets violence
And keeps on causing war.

Someone crept to where they slept
And stole the boys away

372

CYMBELINE

Way back in the mists of time
Augustus ruled in Rome
And Britain's King was Cymbeline
Who reigned back here at home.

He ruled the whole of Britain –
But then his first wife died.
Sad Cymbeline was most distraught,
Oh, how the poor man cried!

But to console and succour him
He had three children fair:
Two boys on whom he showered his love,
A happy boisterous pair,

And a daughter, Imogen,
The oldest of his brood;
And these three children helped to lift
His sad, despondent mood.

The little boys were very young,
Still wanting 'mother's knee';
One was but a baby child,
The other was just three.

But then by most unhappy chance,
On one horrendous day,
Someone crept to where they slept
And stole the boys away.

Although they searched both high and low,
Searched every inch of ground,
The two, sweet, lovely, helpless boys
Were never ever found.

Cymbeline, to ease his grief –
To get another life –
Observed a decent interval,
Then took another wife.

His second marriage wasn't great –
The woman that he chose
Was no sweet, pleasant, caring wife,
She was no English rose.

She was a nasty piece of work,
A scheming, plotting sort,
She brought no calm or happiness
To Cymbeline's great court.

She really hated Imogen,
She thought the girl was crass,
And treated her quite terribly,
Was unfair to the lass.

But though the queen had all this bile
And hatred in her soul,
It didn't change the fact that she
Had one determined goal.

She wished for Imogen to wed
Her own beloved boy;
This was her bold, ambitious plan,
Her very devious ploy.

For she'd been married once before
And at that time she'd had
This son, who was called Cloten –
A most unpleasant lad.

And now she wished the boy to wed
The girl that she put down,
She thought, 'If Cymbeline should die
My boy will get the crown.

'As long as those two little babes
Are never brought back here...
If they were found it would mess up
My clever plan, I fear.'

But as they say, the best laid plans
Can quickly go astray;
Things often have the nerve to go
A very different way.

For Imogen was scheming too,
Plans racing through her head,
And she went off one day and got
Herself, in secret, wed.

Her husband was called Posthumus –
A really decent guy,
A scholar and a gentleman
Who'd always been close by.

His father had died fighting,
A warrior for the cause,
In one of bold King Cymbeline's
Well-planned, but bloody wars.

His wife had then been pregnant
And when the poor girl heard
Of how she'd lost her husband dear
And all that had occurred,

She broke right down with grief and woe,
She pulled her hair – went wild –
And only lived just long enough
To give birth to her child.

The child was friendless in the world –
A baby all alone,
But then good Cymbeline had said,
'I'll raise him as my own.'

He'd called the young babe Posthumus,
'Because this child,' he said,
'Was only born into the world
After his dad was dead.'

And so the youthful Posthumus,
And Imogen there too,
Were taught and played together,
And grew close, as children do.

So by the time they were full-grown
It is not hard to guess,
Their love was all-encompassing,
Complete – and nothing less.

To marry was the natural thing
For this young pair to do,
But it did not take long at all
Before the bad Queen knew.

And then she wasted little time
Before she went to tell
King Cymbeline of what she'd learned –
You should have heard him yell.

He really went quite crazy,
And cried with bitter scorn,
'How could she go and marry
A subject lowly born!'

For though he'd raised the humble lad,
(That surely was one thing.)
It didn't mean the boy could wed
The daughter of a King.

He yelled at youthful Posthumus –
His words were cold and stark –
'You've pushed your luck too far this time,
You've overstepped the mark.

'You're banished now forever,
So leave fair Britain's shore.'
And then with anger in his eyes
He showed the youth the door.

The Queen then said to Imogen –
She whispered in her ear,
'I will arrange a meeting
With your poor husband, dear.'

Whatever was her crafty game?
What now was in her mind?
She thought that if she helped the girl
She very soon would find

That Imogen would trust her
And then she could persuade
The girl to think her marriage
Should quickly be unmade,

'You're banished now forever'

And that, without permission
From the King – her dear old dad,
The marriage was unlawful,
Completely wrong and bad.

So then she could renew her aim
To get the girl to wed
Her darling son, young Cloten.
'I'll sort it out,' she said.

And so the loving pair met up
To say their last goodbyes;
They kissed, embraced and vowed their love
Amid so many sighs.

They gave each other keepsakes:
A bracelet for his wife,
A ring for Posthumus who said,
'I'll wear this ring for life.'

Posthumus departed then,
He left his treasured home
And set his weary way towards
The Continent – then Rome.

And on arrival there he met
A group of brash young chaps,
Fun-loving, pleasure-seeking guys,
A bunch of real madcaps.

They came from different countries
And one day they were praising
The ladies of their own fair lands
In loud, exalted phrasing.

Posthumus of course joined in;
He said, 'Upon my life,
The lady fairest by a mile
Is my sweet, loving wife.'

The lad went on and on until
He said, 'She is the pick
Of all the girls in Britain now.'
He made the others sick.

The more that he continued
The more the young men said
That Posthumus was lying,
That he was off his head.

Then Iachimo, a Roman, vowed,
'However far you roam,
You won't find women to compare
With those who live in Rome.

'To think a girl from Britain
Could ever be compared
With any true-bred Roman lass –
Your judgement is impaired.'

But Posthumus was resolute.
A quarrel soon ensued,
And so a bet was struck upon
To break this angry mood.

'I will go,' said Iachimo,
'To Britain and, once there,
Will make your so-called faithful wife
Transfer her love and care

'To this brave Roman standing here –
I'll show your wife's not true:
As proof I shall bring back to you
Your golden bracelet too.

'And when I hand this to you
You'll surely know one thing:
Your wife has been unfaithful –
So you'll give me her ring.

'And if I'm unsuccessful
I'll give you straight away
A pile of cash in payment...
So now, what do you say?'

Posthumus agreed at once –
He knew his wife was true.
'You'll never win her love,' he said,
'No matter what you do.'

So Iachimo for Britain sailed
To win the prize he sought,
And on arriving went at once
To Cymbeline's proud court.

Made welcome there by Imogen
Because he was a friend,
Of Posthumus, he nonetheless
Gave reason to offend,

For he declared he loved her,
He made it very plain,
But she repulsed him vigorously
With lady-like disdain.

He saw his cause was hopeless,
That Posthumus was right:
She was most faithful, loving, true,
Though he was out of sight.

So then he hit upon a plan,
And, though a rotten trick,
It was a most ingenious scheme,
Quite well thought out and slick.

He bribed the lady's servants –
The wily, devious fox –
To let him hide within her room,
Concealed within a box.

And, hidden in this wooden trunk,
He didn't make a peep,
But waited in there patiently
Till she was fast asleep.

And then he ventured from the trunk,
And, making not a sound,
With notebook and a writing tool,
He took a look around.

He noted all the features
Of Imogen's fine room,
So when he told poor Posthumus
The lad would just assume

He'd been within her chamber
And slept with his sweet dove;
Thus Iachimo could make the claim
That he had won her love.

And then the next thing that he did
Was silently to creep
Towards the bed, within the room
Where she was fast asleep.

And carefully and gingerly
With just a gentle twist
Removed the golden bracelet
From round the sweet girl's wrist.

And then he ventured from the trunk

Then, like a ghost within the night,
This evil rotter slunk
All silently across the room
And got back in the trunk.

Iachimo returned to Rome
And on arriving back
He didn't hang around but rushed
At once to the attack.

He let poor Posthumus have it.
He said, 'Your faithless girl
Did not take much persuading
To let her charms unfurl.'

'It can't be so,' cried Posthumus,
'It really can't be true.
I know my darling Imogen
Would never fancy you.'

But then the evil Iachimo
Described his lady's room;
Hearing this made Posthumus
Sink down in dismal gloom.

But then he brightened up and said,
'That doesn't prove a thing.
Others could have told you this.'
But then there came the sting.

For Iachimo then held aloft
The bracelet o'er his head,
And taunted Posthumus with glee;
'Know you this jewel?' he said.

'Your darling wife gave this to me.
She said there'd been a day
When it had meant a lot to her –
But now to give away

'Was really but a little thing,
So here it is, my friend.'
The anger of poor Posthumus
Was really without end.

He gave the ring to Iachimo,
As he had said he would;
He had no inkling he'd been told
A truly gross falsehood.

But then, consumed by jealous rage,
He wrote to a dear friend,
And said, 'My dear Pisanio,
I wish my wife's swift end.'

He said, 'She has betrayed me
And so she now must die.'
And then he wrote to Imogen
And told her this great lie.

He wrote, 'I'm coming home to you,
I must see you somehow,
Pisanio will tell you where,
So go with him right now.'

She set off with Pisanio then
For Milford Haven town,
But on the way Pisanio said
With many a troubled frown,

'Your husband wants your death, but I
Cannot perform this task;
It really is a cruel request,
Not something he should ask.'

On hearing this she said, 'I can't
Think now of coming home.'
And so she dressed up as a man
Intent on reaching Rome.

For though her husband wished her dead
She still adored him so,
And thus she set off there and then
To seek her love, her beau.

Before she went, Pisanio said,
'Please take this phial, I pray,
For it contains a remedy
Which you may need one day.

'It is a cure for everything,
According to the Queen.
She gave it to me saying
It's the best there's ever been.'

(The Queen detests Pisanio
Because he is so close
To Imogen and Posthumus –
She hopes he'll take a dose.

For she believes it poison –
But it is just a potion
That brings about a deathlike sleep
And stifles breath and motion.)

So Imogen went on her way,
The potion in her care.
She journeyed through a forest wild,
And then got lost in there.

She stumbled round and round until,
With fear etched on her face,
She came upon a sort of house,
A very humble place.

For it was but a dismal cave,
A sorry little dwelling,
And who might live within this place
There really was no telling.

With trepidation in her heart,
But trying to look brave,
She took a deep and bracing breath
And walked into the cave.

And there she found to her delight
A choice, lean side of meat;
And then without a 'by your leave'
She sat right down to eat.

The cave was someone else's home,
But she was tired and weak,
So ate their food without a thought –
She really had a cheek.

I think an explanation
Would be in order here,
Because the owners of this home
From hunting now draw near.

One is called Belarius,
A man who once had been
A much respected noble at
The court of Cymbeline.

A sorry little dwelling

But he had falsely been accused
Of plotting highest treason –
Someone had made the whole thing up
For no apparent reason.

Belarius had been so hurt
And angry through and through
That in a vengeful moment
He'd decided what to do.

He'd stolen Cymbeline's two sons;
His purpose was to make
The King a lonely, desperate man
And make his poor heart break.

And this, of course, is what occurred
As we've already seen:
Cymbeline was as distraught
As anyone has been.

Belarius had brought the boys,
(Oh, such a naughty knave),
Into the forest – made a home
Within the dismal cave.

And though he'd stolen these two lads
For vengeance – that alone –
He soon had learnt to care for them
And love them as his own.

He taught them lessons, how to hunt
And fish with hook and line,
And so they grew into young men
Both noble, fit and fine.

One was called Guiderius –
Arviragus, the other,
But Belarius changed the names
Of each imperial brother.

Guiderius was now renamed
As Polydore – and then
He called Arviragus, Cadwal;
And so these two young men

Had not the least suspicion of
Their high and princely worth;
They had no thought that they were each
Of noble, royal birth.

So back now to the story –
Belarius returns
With his reputed sons, and now
He straightaway discerns

A visitor is in the cave.
'Whoever's this?' he cries.
'It surely is an angel that
I see before my eyes.'

For though poor Imogen was dressed
As if she were a boy,
She still looked very comely,
Appealing, sweet and coy.

'Please don't harm me,' she cried out,
'Here's money for the meat.
I'm sorry that I took so much
But I just had to eat.

'And if you choose to kill me
For taking meat today,
Then you should know, without the food
I'd be dead anyway.'

Belarius asked, 'What is your name?
And where is it you're going?'
'Fidele,' she then answered him.
They had no way of knowing

Who she really was and how
She'd ended up right there.
'I head for Italy,' she said,
'At least that is my prayer.'

Belarius replied, 'Fair youth,
Don't hurry from our sight.
You truly are most welcome here,
So stay with us tonight.

'And do not judge us by this place
For though we seem low-born,
Who live in this poor lowly cave,
Cut off, bereft, careworn,

'We are much more than first we seem...
I beg you, have no fear,
Come, be our guest and stay awhile,
You're very welcome here.'

So Imogen remained with them
And very quickly found
A closeness with the brothers –
They liked having her around.

Of course they called her Fidele –
They thought she was a boy.
They were completely taken in
By Imogen's sly ploy.

But then one day the boys declared
A-hunting they would go,
Fidele said she wasn't well,
That she was feeling low.

And so they left her on her own
But once they'd gone away,
A bright idea occurred to her
To help her through that day.

She thought, 'I'll feel much better if
I take some of the potion
Pisanio kindly gave to me.'
Of course she had no notion

Of what the cordial contained –
The sorrow she would reap;
And drinking it she then fell down
Into a deathlike sleep.

Belarius and the brothers,
Returning from their trip
Believed that young Fidele
Was having just a kip.

But when *he* neither breathed nor moved
They cried in great confusion,
And that the lad was dead and gone
Was swiftly their conclusion.

It was such a sorry thing,
The brothers were so sad –
Just as they'd come to know him well
They'd lost the lovely lad.

They carried Imogen with care
Into a shady glade
And lovingly, with gentleness,
There Imogen was laid.

And lovingly, with gentleness,
There Imogen was laid

They covered her with leaves and flowers
And said a little prayer,
Then with sad hearts and many tears
They left the body there.

But very soon the girl awoke;
She gave a little cough,
She rubbed her eyes and cleared her throat –
The drug was wearing off.

Then she exclaimed in startled tone,
'Now how did I get here?
This mound all strewn with fragrant flowers
Seems like a funeral bier.

'I thought I'd found some helpful friends,
But now it surely seems
That they were but imagined –
A figment of my dreams.'

So once again she set her path
Away from hearth and home,
To Milford Haven and from there
She'd board a ship for Rome.

Meanwhile a war had broken out,
Ferociously between
Rome's Emperor, Augustus,
And Britain's Cymbeline.

A Roman army now advanced
Right through the very wood
In which the fleeing Imogen,
Unknowingly, now stood.

And with the army came a man
Of grace and bold hauteur –
It was her husband Posthumus
Who meant so much to her.

But though he was surrounded
By all the Roman might,
He was determined it would be
For Britain he would fight.

And though King Cymbeline had said,
'You're banished from this land.'
It was to him that he was set
To give a helping hand.

He thought his Imogen was dead –
Pisanio had sent
A note that said he'd killed the girl,
And though he did repent

Of asking him to kill his wife,
Now nothing could be done;
He simply yearned for death because
He felt his course was run.

He'd lose his life in battle,
Embroiled in an attack,
Or Cymbeline would kill him
For daring to come back.

And so a battle then commenced
'Twixt Rome and Britain's force,
And Fortune seemed to favour Rome
As battle took its course.

Belarius and the King's two sons
Had joined the army too;
The three of them all thought it was
The decent thing to do.

Then, with amazing bravery,
Posthumus at the scene,
Along with good Belarius
And the sons of Cymbeline,

They turned the battle round and saved
The life of Britain's King;
It was the most astounding act,
A really marvellous thing.

They turned the battle round

Their actions saved the battle
And put Rome's force to flight,
It was a glorious victory,
A quite amazing sight.

But what of lonely Imogen?
What happened to the lass?
Well, she had been surrounded
By the Romans in a mass.

She had been taken prisoner
And forced to serve as page
To one of Rome's fine generals
For but a paltry wage.

The fight then over, Imogen
A *Roman* too it seemed
Was taken prisoner by the Brits
For no-one present deemed

She was the Princess in disguise
(Well, how were they to see?)
And so she waited there with hope
That soon they'd set her free.

And with her stood the general
Whom she'd been forced to serve.
Lucius was the general's name,
A man of steel and nerve.

And Iachimo, a prisoner too,
Was brought to Cymbeline,
And Posthumus, now taken,
Was summoned to the scene.

So they all stood there waiting for
Their fate to be made known,
Posthumus now thought for sure,
His cover being blown,

That he would soon be put to death –
It's what the King would rule –
To hope for any mercy
Would be to act the fool.

And then Belarius came in
And with him standing there,
The two brave sons of Cymbeline –
Oh, such a handsome pair.

They came to gain their just reward
For how the three had striven
To save the King and for the help
And service they had given.

And also with the King was found
Pisanio as well;
He was the King's attendant and
Saw all that then befell.

They waited there in silence,
Before the King they knelt,
Each with his different hopes and fears
Dividing how they felt.

Imogen gazed at Posthumus,
And saw her heart's desire.
He didn't recognise her dressed
In all her male attire.

But then she spotted Iachimo –
This man of course she knew –
But didn't know as yet he'd been
So false and so untrue:

The author of her broken heart.
But then the strangest thing –
She saw upon his finger there
Her own beloved ring.

She gasped a little to herself;
She really must learn more,
But it was hard while she remained
A prisoner of war.

Pisanio looked at Imogen
And in a tick surmised
Just who she was, despite the fact
She was so well disguised.

For he had been the one to help
Her dress up as a boy,
He'd been the willing architect
Of this her crafty ploy.

Belarius then spoke these words,
In whispers to his son:
'Cadwal, is that not Fidele?
I'm sure that he's the one

'We found that day within our cave,
Who subsequently died.'
'He looks the same, without a doubt,'
His faithful *son* replied.

'If it were he, he would speak out,'
Belarius then said.
'He'd say a friendly word to us –
Fidele must be dead.'

Posthumus stood there silently,
Determined he'd not say
How he had helped to save the King
On that auspicious day.

He wished no pardon for his pains –
No kingly act of grace;
He'd welcome death and run to it,
A smile upon his face.

The Roman general, Lucius
Was first of them to speak.
It must be said he truly thought
His future looked most bleak.

'I've heard it told,' he bravely said,
'That you, King Cymbeline,
Will ransom no poor prisoners,
For vengeance must be seen.

'You sentence all you catch to death,
And so I boldly say
I'll gladly suffer death from you,
But in a Roman way.

'And I would ask but one small thing,
And beg you to engage
Your kindly virtues and to spare
This young boy here – my page.

'He is a Briton by his birth
And I must truly stress
It wasn't by his doing
That he wound up in this mess.

'He was taken prisoner
And therefore had no choice
Except to do as he was told;
He really had no voice.

'And he has proved to be as true
As any Roman lad.
The boy is kind and dutiful,
The best I've ever had.

'And yes, he served a Roman,
Though not for very long,
But I can say with certainty,
He did no Briton wrong.'

When Cymbeline took in these words
And saw his daughter fair,
Of course he didn't recognise
The girl disguised right there,

But something of her presence
Moved him in such a way
That with all kingly grace and charm
He had these words to say:

'I spare your life, young gracious boy,
And then another thing –
You may ask any favour
From me, your noble King.'

Said Imogen, 'Thank you, my Lord.'
And Lucius then spoke;
He thought his page would speak for him
And save him at a stroke.

He said, 'I do not beg my life,
But know it's this you'll crave.'
She said, 'I've other work to do,
Your life I cannot save.'

The general was amazed, it's true,
By such a surly mood;
He thought her action really showed
A gross ingratitude.

Then Imogen made her request.
She said, 'I wish to know
How Iachimo came by that ring.'
He had nowhere to go.

And so he there and then confessed,
He broke into a sweat,
And then he told them how he'd lied
And all about the bet.

When Posthumus heard him confess
That Imogen was true,
He told the court just what he'd asked
Pisanio to do.

He utterly broke down and cried,
'I took the sweet girl's life.
Oh, Imogen, my Queen, my love,
Oh, Imogen – my wife!'

When Imogen saw his distress
It broke her heart in two.
She threw off her disguise and cried,
'My husband – I love you!'

Then Posthumus was quite amazed –
Could not believe his eyes;
And all the court on seeing this
Burst out in happy cries.

King Cymbeline was overwhelmed,
It filled his soul with awe...
What a gracious gift from God
To find his girl once more.

But there was more for Cymbeline
To turn his fuddled head:
Belarius stepped forward,
'I beg your ear,' he said.

And then he told the King his tale,
Of everything he'd done,
And then he said, 'Here is your boy,
And here, your other son.'

The King could not contain himself,
He knew not what to do –
Guiderius stepped forward
And Aviragus too.

The King embraced the pair of them,
His love just knew no end;
Then to Belarius he said,
'I once called you my friend –

'And it shall be so once again,
For though you were a knave,
I here and now do pardon you.'
And then the King forgave.

Then Imogen said, 'Father dear,
Will you now heed my pleas?
Will you spare General Lucius?
I'm begging on my knees.'

Cymbeline agreed and said,
'Now let all warfare cease,
And I propose that with great Rome
We shall conclude a peace.'

And thus it was, surrounded by
A flood of happy tears,
A peace with Rome was made, which then
Was kept for many years.

And so it ended happily,
But one thing must be said,
And that is to recount the fact
The evil Queen was dead.

She died borne down with deep despair –
Her plans had gone astray –
But also touched by some remorse
She thus had passed away.

So with the loss of his bad wife,
This evil, scheming Queen,
There was nothing left to mar
The joy of Cymbeline.

In gratitude for how things were,
How could he ask for more?
He recognised young Posthumus
As his new son-in-law.

And Cymbeline for many years
Stood at Britannia's helm;
He ruled with great compassion
Across a peaceful realm.

In quite the finest set of clothes
The court had ever seen

HENRY THE EIGHTH

Our story opens at the court
Of Henry – England's King –
And there we find three Lords who speak
Of a momentous thing.

Their royal master, Henry,
The eighth that England's had,
Has just come back from France, where he –
The vain man – had been clad

In quite the finest set of clothes
The court had ever seen;
The meeting was most dazzling,
The showiest there'd been.

For there the young King Henry
And France's young King too,
Competed with each other.
They each tried to outdo

The other with their finery,
The splendour of their court.
And in amongst the glitter
There was much fun and sport.

This meeting has grown famous;
You may have heard it told
How these two Kings met at the field
Known as the Cloth of Gold.

For there was such great opulence
And splendour all on show;
Everything was bright and brash,
The whole field was a-glow

With shiny, sparkling armour
Bedecking men so bold;
And pennants flying in the breeze
Of red and blue and gold.

And in amongst this dazzling sight
Two Kings had walked abroad,
Dressed in their lavish finery
They walked on that green sward.

Their garments had so glittered –
A sight there to behold.
That's why this pageant has been called
The Field of Cloth of Gold.

But as the Lords there chat away,
Says Buckingham, 'Perchance,
This was too much extravagance,
Just for a chat with France.

'It cost a lot of money,
We went right over-board.'
But Norfolk said, 'If I were you
I'd watch your tongue, my Lord.

'For Wolsey, Henry's Cardinal,
He organised the thing,
And, as you know, he's very close
And friendly with the King.'

Buckingham says Wolsey
Is always on the make;
Though he pretends great piety
He's really on the take.

'It's time the King was made aware
That Wolsey is a crook –
His two-faced lying attitude
Is something I'll not brook.'

He thinks, 'I'll tell King Henry
Of the man's dishonesty,
And then, with luck, in gratitude
The King will honour me.'

Before the Duke of Buckingham
Can put his plan in place,
He is accused of treason,
Arrested in disgrace.

The Cardinal's behind it –
And not without good reason:
He's set to get revenge and so
Accuses him of treason.

And though a trial's soon arranged,
It all becomes quite clear
That Henry wants him dead as well,
And will not deign to hear

Lord Buckingham's defence and so
The Duke is in a jam,
The court proceedings are absurd
The trial just a sham.

And so he was condemned – and then
Beheading was his fate,
For gross disloyalty towards
The King and to the state.

As he was led away to die –
Beheading on the block,
Poor Buckingham looked back on things
And gravely he took stock.

He spoke aloud most earnestly
And said, 'I'd have you know
That those who come to pity me,
Just hear these words then go.

'I have this day received the word,
A traitor, I must die,
But I declare in Heaven's name
This judgement is a lie.

'And even as the axe comes down
Depriving me of breath,
I do swear that I do bear
No malice for my death.

'And to those few who loved me –
To those who showed me care –
I ask that as the axe-man strikes
You offer up a prayer.

'And with this one sweet sacrifice
Whispered in words so soft,
You will assist the angels as
They bear my soul aloft.

'And now I say of Henry,
He made me a worthy man,
He bore me up to noble things
As only great kings can.

'But at a stroke, he cast me down
And put this friend on trial,
Accused of treason and though false,
He will brook no denial.

'Yet as I stand so close to death,
I see his regal face,
And beg that if you see the King,
Commend me to his Grace.

'But now good people, I must leave
This world where pain runs rife,
For I must face the final hour
Of my long, weary life.

'And when of something that is sad
You would to others tell,
Then speak of how Lord Buckingham
Met his sad fate and fell.'

And then he said, 'Forgive me God.'
Then turned to everyone
And sadly breathed his last goodbye,
'Farewell, for now I'm done.'

Queen Katherine, the King's good wife,
Thinks ill of Wolsey too.
She says, 'He's full of grasping greed,
Corrupt and false right through.'

And so against these goings-on
The king arrives to play;
A banquet and a splendid ball
Are taking place that day.

He enters and he walks around
And then, as if by chance,
He looks across at Anne Boleyn
With a romantic glance.

Lady-in-waiting to the queen,
She stands demurely there.
She shouldn't flirt with Henry,
She really should take care.

But then what can she do when he,
The King of everyone,
Winks and then commands that she
Should dance and have some fun.

So now the King has let his gaze
Fall lustfully upon
Young Anne Boleyn and he's about
To pull an awful con.

For Henry now decides to say,
'The Queen is not my wife.
I cannot carry on this way
And live this sinful life.

'My brother was her husband once –
I now see all along,
Though he is dead, for us to wed
Was absolutely wrong.'

But this, of course, was just a ruse,
A way to make the claim
His marriage was a living lie –
Divorce was now his aim.

The papal legate comes from Rome.
The King hopes he'll endorse
His claim that Katherine's not his wife,
And grant him a divorce.

He hopes he'll say that when he wed
His brother's wife before,
The Pope will undertake to state
He broke the Church's law.

That he's not really married to
Queen Katherine, that he
Was wrong to take his brother's wife,
Though she was by then free.

So Henry argued furiously
And with tremendous force
His marriage wasn't legal;
They therefore must divorce.

And thus a public trial is called –
Queen Katherine pleads her case.
There is great sadness and disdain
Upon the good Queen's face.

She says she is the rightful wife
Of royal Henry there.
She says, 'The way he's treating me
Is totally unfair.

'For, Heaven witness, I've been true
Through all upsets and strife;
I've always been most dutiful,
A true and humble wife.

'So how have I offended?'
Her voice was strained and shrill.
'I've always been compliant
And faithful to his will.

'And so I say, my Lord, to you,
Why do you cause this fuss?
Why do you drag me here to court
And make such fools of us?

'I've been your faithful, loving wife
Through ups and downs and tears.
And lived in strict obedience
For nigh on twenty years.

'And when at first we spoke our vows,
Upon our wedding day,
Did not those present all declare
It lawful – speak I pray.

'For my dear father, King of Spain,
And your good father too,
Both took wise counsel everywhere
Of what was right to do.

'And all spoke out and did proclaim
It was within the law.
So tell me Henry, husband dear,
What is this trial for?'

And then in desperation
She said, 'My only hope
Is to appeal to Rome itself,
To beg help from the Pope.'

A silence fell upon the court,
An all-pervading gloom,
And then Queen Katherine rose and stormed
In anger from the room.

'So tell me Henry, husband dear,
What is this trial for?'

The papal legate sighed and said,
As he surveyed the scene,
'We cannot carry on without
The presence of the Queen.'

And so that seemed the end of it.
King Henry sighed as well:
'She never was my legal wife...'
What lies this man could tell!

⁂

Now Wolsey, that old crafty fox,
Had plans that were his own.
He wanted young King Henry
To share the English throne

With a lady who was sister
To France's noble King,
He thought that this would prove to be
An advantageous thing.

But now King Henry was in love
With Anne Boleyn and so
There was not any chance at all
That he would want to know.

When Wolsey saw this was the case,
He thought, 'I won't endorse
His marriage plans' – so asked the Pope
To turn down the divorce.

His devious note was found, alas,
And taken with all haste
Unto the King, who looked at it
With evident distaste.

He asks poor Wolsey to declare
He's loyal and he's true.
Wolsey replies, 'Your highness knows,
I've always toiled for you.'

The King replied, 'You lie to me,
For Wolsey – with great stealth,
You've lined your pockets o'er the years
And so amassed great wealth.

'I've seen a list of all you own,'
The King then archly mocked.
'And I must tell you Cardinal
Your monarch's deeply shocked.

'These papers fell into my hands,
They're here for you to see,
They clearly show that you have not
Been looking out for me.

'You've filled your own great coffers –
You can read it all in here.'
Wolsey thought, 'Is this the end
Of my acclaimed career?'

But when he's shown the letter
That he'd written to the Pope
He sees the game is truly up;
He gives up any hope,

And says, 'I've touched the highest post
My shoes will ever fill.
I see that from this glorious point
The way's now all downhill.'

He never spoke a truer word –
The King gave him the sack.
He said, 'Get out of here, right now,
And don't you dare come back.'

That was the end of Wolsey:
He left with downcast head,
And shortly after this they heard
The poor old guy was dead.

The King gave him the sack

Henry now divorced his Queen
His wife he just denied;
With ruthlessness the Tudor King
Threw Katherine aside.

And then he married Anne Boleyn –
The King had got his way,
And he arranged for her to have
A coronation day.

And it was said that Anne Boleyn
Looked quite the comely Queen,
As gracious, fair and beautiful
As any woman seen.

And when the people looked on her
'Twas said by everyone
It truly was a noble thing
Their monarch had now done.

And such a mighty cheer rose up
That shook the very clouds,
A noise just like a tempest makes
Within a ship's great shrouds.

Hats and coats and doublets all
Were thrown into the air.
It was a truly happy day,
A joyful, fun affair.

At length young Anne Boleyn approached,
Serene and with restraint
Unto the alter where she prayed,
She looked just like a saint.

She gazed up to the heavens,
And then she prayed again,
And all the people were as one
In hoping she would reign,

For many long and fruitful years –
They hoped she'd always be
Beside their monarch – there to give
Support and company.

Then Canterbury's archbishop,
Who was presiding there
Bestowed the royal emblems
As he pronounced a prayer.

Edward Confessor's crown came first,
The rod and bird of peace,
Then holy oil anointed her –
And then an ermine fleece.

The choir sang *Te Deum*,
The music was the best.
It stirred the soul and roused the blood
Of every noble guest.

Then once she was declared the Queen
By Canterbury's priest,
The wedding party all repaired
To York Place for a feast.

So Anne was Queen – but Katherine now
Was sick and close to death.
She wrote to Henry desperately,
And said, 'With my last breath,

'I beg you treat our daughter,
Young Mary, with respect;
Maintain her in the proper way
A princess should expect.'

And then she said, 'Dear Henry,
I now bid you goodbye.
Be certain in the knowledge that
I bless you as I die.'

Queen Anne is now in labour.
And then, one early morn,
A little baby daughter
Most happily is born.

The court comes for the christening;
They give their thanks and pray
For Henry's royal baby and
For this momentous day.

Archbishop Cranmer says to all:
'Be of good cheer, I pray.
A thousand, thousand blessings
This child brings us today.

'She brings unto this land of ours
Redemption from above,
Great peace and plenty, truth and joy,
Great harmony and love.'

King Henry really beamed at that;
He couldn't get enough
Of all this gilded flattery
And highfalutin stuff.

He then stood up and cried aloud,
Emotions all a-fire,
'When I'm in Heaven I declare
That all I shall desire,

'Will be to gaze upon this child.
I know I'll get a buzz –
I'll be so full of eagerness
To see what this child does!'

Prophetic words, it must be said:
In time the girl became
A truly great and much loved Queen,
For she went by the name

Elizabeth of England,
The first the realm had known.
For many happy, prosperous years
She'd sit on England's throne.

But that was in the future.
Now, as King Henry sighed,
The future Queen Elizabeth
Lay in her crib and cried.

Complete your collection with the other books in this series:

Easy Reading Shakespeare Volume One contains

The Merchant of Venice

Much Ado About Nothing

The Tempest

Hamlet, Prince of Denmark

Macbeth

Twelfth Night

Romeo and Juliet

Othello

King Lear

A Midsummer Night's Dream

Easy Reading Shakespeare Volume Two contains

The Taming of the Shrew

Measure for Measure

Julius Caesar

Antony and Cleopatra

As You Like It

Henry the Fourth – Parts I and II

Henry the Fifth

The Winter's Tale

Richard the Third

The Two Gentlemen of Verona

All's Well That Ends Well